NEW Challenges

Amanda Maris

Workbook 1

Contents

Get Ready

A You 3
B Your Family 4
C Your Classroom 6
D Your School 7
E Your Room 9
F Your Photos 10

Module 1 The Challenge

Get Ready 11
1 Vocabulary and Grammar 12
2 Vocabulary and Grammar 14
3 Skills 16
Language Check 1 18

Module 2 Exercise

Get Ready 19
4 Vocabulary and Grammar 20
5 Vocabulary and Grammar 22
6 Skills 24
Reading Corner 1 26
Language Check 2 28

Module 3 Risk

Get Ready 29
7 Vocabulary and Grammar 30
8 Vocabulary and Grammar 32
9 Skills 34
Language Check 3 36

Module 4 Out and About

Get Ready 37
10 Vocabulary and Grammar 38
11 Vocabulary and Grammar 40
12 Skills 42
Reading Corner 2 44
Language Check 4 46

Module 5 The Weather

Get Ready 47
13 Vocabulary and Grammar 48
14 Vocabulary and Grammar 50
15 Skills 52
Language Check 5 54

Module 6 Expeditions

Get Ready 55
16 Vocabulary and Grammar 56
17 Vocabulary and Grammar 58
18 Skills 60
Reading Corner 3 62
Language Check 6 64

Module 7 Helping

Get Ready 65
19 Vocabulary and Grammar 66
20 Vocabulary and Grammar 68
21 Skills 70
Language Check 7 72

Module 8 Television

Get Ready 73
22 Vocabulary and Grammar 74
23 Vocabulary and Grammar 76
24 Skills 78
Reading Corner 4 80
Language Check 8 82

Wordlist 83
Grammar Reference 87

You

Vocabulary: Countries/Nationalities

1 **Complete the names of the countries. Use *a*, *e*, *i*, *o* or *u*.**

1 J *a* p *a* n
2 P _ rt _ g _ l
3 th _ _ n _ t _ d K _ ngd _ m
4 _ rg _ nt _ n _
5 Gr _ _ c _
6 R _ ss _ _
7 th _ _ n _ t _ d St _ t _ s
8 T _ rk _ y
9 C _ n _ d _

2 **Complete the table with nationality adjectives from the countries in Exercise 1.**

Word Builder

-ese	*Japanese*	______
-ish	______	______
-an / -ian	______	______
	______	______
other	______	

3 **Choose the correct words.**

1 Are you *Brazil* / *(Brazilian)*?
2 My friend is from *Spain* / *Spanish*.
3 Are you *Australian* / *Australia*?
4 Where are you from? *Chinese* / *China*.
5 Fabio Capello is *Italy* / *Italian*.
6 I'm from *Poland* / *Polish*.

Grammar: *to be*

➤ Grammar Reference, page 87

☆ **4** **Correct the mistakes.**

1 My teacher (are) from London. *is*
2 My friend (no is) Spanish. ______
3 I (is) a student. ______
4 (Are) he a teacher? ______
5 We (isn't) American. ______
6 Where (is) they from? ______
7 Sally and John (is) from New York. ______
8 Are you from Japan? Yes, (I'm). ______

☆ **5** **Complete the dialogue with the correct form of *to be*.**

A Hello. My name [1]*'s* ______ Lucy Hill. I [2]______ your teacher.
B Hello.
A What [3]______ your name?
B Mark. I [4]______ from Australia.
A [5]______ you from Sydney?
B No, I [6]______ not. I [7]______ from Melbourne.
A And [8]______ your friends Australian, too?
B No, they [9]______. Isabel [10]______ Brazilian and Dan [11]______ American. What nationality [12]______ you, Miss Hill?
A I [13]______ Canadian.

☆ **6** **Match (1–5) and (a–e) to make questions.**

1 Are you — b
2 What's
3 What nationality are
4 Where are
5 What nationality is

a you from?
b a teacher?
c your name?
d your teacher?
e your friends?

Your Turn

☆☆ **7** **Write true answers to the questions in Exercise 6.**

1 ______________________ .
2 ______________________ .
3 ______________________ .
4 ______________________ .
5 ______________________ .

Key Expressions: Meeting people

8 **Number the lines of the dialogue.**

A Hello. [1]
B Loukas. Nice to meet you. [ ]
A Where are you from? [ ]
B Hi. [ ]
A I'm from Shanghai. [ ]
B Athens, and you? [ ]
A My name's Lin. What's your name? [ ]

B Your Family

Vocabulary: Numbers

1 **Write the numbers next to the correct words.**

1	5	11	13	24	30
46	52	~~61~~	79	87	99

a	*61*	sixty-one	**g**		one
b		eleven	**h**		forty-six
c		twenty-four	**i**		thirteen
d		seventy-nine	**j**		thirty
e		fifty-two	**k**		eighty-seven
f		ninety-nine	**l**		five

2 **Complete the numbers with *-teen* or *-ty*.**

Word Builder

13	thir *teen*	70	seven______
40	for______	15	fif______
19	nine______	60	six______
90	nine______	18	eigh______

Vocabulary: Family

3 **Complete the description of Fiona's family.**

Hi. My name's Fiona and I'm [1] *fourteen*. Angela is my [2] ______ and she's [3] ______. My [4] ______, James, is sixty-three. My mother and [5] ______ are called Rachel and Joe. Mum is [6] ______ and Dad is forty. My [7] ______ is called Chris and he's [8] ______. My aunt, Claire, and my [9] ______, Tim, are great. My [10] ______ is called Daniel and he's [11] ______.

4 **Read about the people from the family tree in Exercise 3. Who are they?**

1 My cousin and I are both twelve. His mum and dad are called Claire and Tim. *Chris*
2 I'm thirty-five. My son is twelve. ______
3 My sister is thirty-eight and I'm thirty-six. ______
4 My favourite grandson is twelve. My daughter is thirty-eight and I'm sixty-one. ______

Your Turn

5 **Write about four people in your family.**
My brother is called Adam. He's seventeen.

1 ______.
2 ______.
3 ______.
4 ______.

Vocabulary: Ordinal numbers/ months

6 Find eight ordinal numbers. Then write them in order.

twenty-ninthfifteenthfirstthirty-firstseventhsecondtenthtwentieth

first, ______________________

7 Complete the crossword.

Across

~~3 the twelfth month~~
6 the seventh month
9 the ninth month
10 the first month
11 the eleventh month

Down

1 the tenth month
2 the fifth month
4 the third month
5 the eighth month
7 the second month
8 the fourth month
10 the sixth month

Grammar: Possessive adjectives/'s

➤ Grammar Reference, page 87

☆ 8 Choose the correct words.

1 My name's Helen. (*I*) / *My* am twenty-one.
2 Your dog is great. What's *it's* / *its* name?
3 My children are English. *They* / *Their* grandfather is American.
4 I am twelve and my sister is fourteen. *We* / *Our* grandmother is seventy.
5 My husband is Spanish. *His* / *Her* name is Enrique.
6 What nationality is *you* / *your* teacher?
7 My aunt is a teacher. *His* / *Her* school is in Manchester.

☆ 9 Complete the text with the words in the box.

their his her (x2) ~~my~~ our

My name's Jasmine. [1] *My* mum's name is Liz. She's English and [2] ______ family is from London. My dad is called Faruk. He isn't English – he's Turkish. [3] ______ family is from Istanbul. My brother and I are English *and* Turkish! [4] ______ cousins in Istanbul are great. [5] ______ mum is my favourite aunt. [6] ______ name is Leyla.

☆ 10 Look at the underlined words. Tick the correct box.

		is	possessive *'s*
1	Vicky's in Class 3.	✓	
2	Li's mum is from China.		✓
3	Helen's my sister.		
4	My friend's teacher is from Poland.		
5	My brother's nineteen.		
6	His dad's name is Ricardo.		

☆ 11 Look at the underlined words. Write S (Singular) or P (Plural).

1 The teacher's name is Miss Clarke. *S*
2 The children's favourite aunt is called Amy. *P*
3 James's new dog is great. ☐
4 My parents' names are Eddie and Jill. ☐
5 My sisters' school is in London. ☐
6 Our cousin's dad is from Spain. ☐

Your Turn

☆☆ 12 Complete the text with true information.

1 My name is ______ .
I'm ______ . ______ birthday is on ______ .

2 My friend's name is ______ .
______ is ______ . ______ birthday is on ______ .

3 My ______ name is ______ .
______ is ______ . ______ birthday is on ______ .

Vocabulary: Classroom objects

1 Look at the picture and write the correct numbers.

board	*1*	desk		pen	
chair		ruler		books	
cupboard		DVD player		plant	
bookshelf		dictionary		bin	

2 Complete the puzzle with the names of the objects in Exercise 1. What's the mystery word?

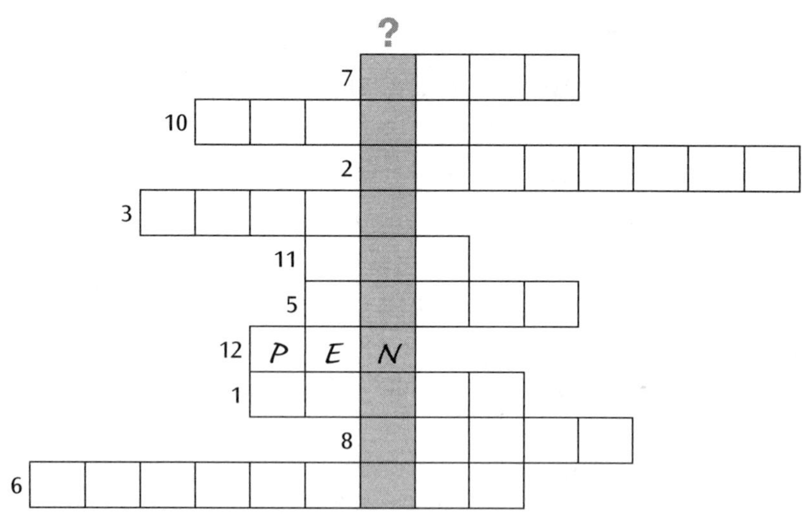

3 Complete the table.

Word Builder

~~bag~~ woman class wife man dictionary watch wall bookshelf window person child box pen

	Plural			
add *s*	*bags*	_____	_____	_____
add *es*	_____	_____	_____	
change *y* to *ies*	_____			
change *f* to *ves*	_____	_____		
irregular	_____	_____	_____	_____

Grammar: Prepositions of place

➤ Grammar Reference, page 88

☆ **4 Look at the picture in Exercise 1. Complete the sentences with the prepositions in the box.**

~~under~~ next to behind in on between in front of

1 The bookshelf is *under* the window.
2 The cupboard is ________ the poster.
3 The dictionary is ________ the desk.
4 The box of pencils is ________ the plant.
5 The TV is ________ the cupboard.
6 The board is ________ the poster.
7 The watch is ________ the pen and the pencil.

☆ **5 What is it?**

1 They're in the bookshelf. the *books*
2 It's under the window. the ________
3 It's on the wall, next to the poster. the ________
4 It's on the student's desk, next to the dictionary. the ________
5 It's next to the door. the ________

D Your School

Vocabulary: School subjects

1 **Complete the names of the school subjects.**

a *a r t* ☐
b g _ _ g _ _ _ _ _ ☐
c E _ _ _ _ _ h ☐
d _ h _ _ _ c _ _ e _ _ _ a _ _ _ _ (P.E.) ☐
e m _ t _ _ ☐
f _ c _ _ _ c _ ☐
g _ i _ _ _ _ y ☐
h _ _ s i _ ☐
i _ _ _ n _ _ e ☐
j _ n _ _ _ _ a _ _ o _
t _ _ h _ _ _ _ _ _ y (IT) ☐

2 **Number the school subjects in Exercise 1 from 1 to 10 (1 = your favourite subject).**

Key Expressions: Telling the time

3 **Write the times in words and numbers.**

1 *twelve o'clock* *12.00*

2 ______

3 ______

4 ______

5 ______

6 ______

7 ______

8 ______

Vocabulary: Days

4 **Write the days in the correct order.**

1 *Monday*
2 ______
3 ______
4 ______
5 ______
6 ______
7 ______

Your Turn

5 **Write the days for these birthdays.**

1 my birthday ______
2 my friend ______
3 my mum ______
4 my dad ______
5 my grandmother ______

6 **Write true sentences about your timetable.**

P.E. / day / time
P.E. is on Wednesday at quarter past two.

1 break / time ______
2 maths / day / time ______
3 history / day / time ______
4 lunch / time ______
5 English / day / time ______
6 science / day / time ______

Grammar: Imperatives

➤ Grammar Reference, page 89

☆ **7** **Complete the instructions with the words in the box.**

don't write ~~look at~~ don't speak open listen to don't sit down

1 *Look at* the poster.

2 ________ the dialogue.

3 ________ on the board.

4 ________ to your partner in the lesson.

5 ________ the window.

6 ________ in the PE lesson.

☆☆ **8** **Complete the poster.**

Be a good English student

- ________ English every day.
- ________ books in English.
- ________ your language in the English class.
- ________ English singers.
- ________ new words in your English notebook.

Grammar: Object pronouns

➤ Grammar Reference, page 89

☆ **9** **Choose the correct words.**

1. Read the question and tell (*me*) / *you* the answer.
2. Listen to the words on the CD. Then repeat *it* / *them*.
3. My name's Ann. Tell *me* / *I* your name.
4. My aunt is Spanish. Ask *him* / *her* about Madrid.
5. My brother is a teacher. Ask *him* / *her* for help.
6. We're new at this school. Tell *them* / *us* about the teachers.
7. This CD is great. Listen to *it* / *her*.

☆☆ **10** **Complete the dialogue with the correct object pronouns.**

Teacher Sit down, please, students.

Students Yes, Miss Clarke.

Teacher Simon, tell [1] *me* the date, please.

Simon It's the second of June.

Teacher Good. Emily, write [2] ________ on the board, please.

Emily Yes, Miss.

Teacher Good. Open your books on page 27. Look at the picture of the woman and read about [3] ________ . Then answer the questions in your notebook.

Mark Emily, tell [4] ________ the answers.

Teacher Mark, please don't speak to Emily. Don't ask [5] ________ for help. Ask me.

Mark OK, Miss.

E Your Room

Vocabulary: Objects in your bedroom

1 Look at the picture and write the names of the objects in the bedroom.

1. It's between the window and desk. bed
2. It's next to the window. w________
3. It's under all the objects. c________
4. It's on the desk. c________
5. They're in front of the chair. C________
6. It's on the bed. m________
7. It's on the shelf. C________
8. It's next to the computer. l________

Your Turn

2 What's in your bedroom? Write five things.

1. ____________
2. ____________
3. ____________
4. ____________
5. ____________

Vocabulary: Colours

3 Write the colours.

1. red + green = brown
2. black + ________ = grey
3. red + white = ________
4. ________ + blue = purple
5. red + yellow = ________
6. yellow + ________ = green

Your Turn

4 Write about your bedroom.

The ________ (object) is next to my bed. My ________ (object) ________ on the desk. My poster of ________ (person) is on the wall. My CDs are ________ (place). My curtains are ________ (colour) and the carpet is ________ (colour).

Grammar: *this, that, these, those*

➤ Grammar Reference, page 89

☆ **5 Complete the sentences with *this*, *that*, *these* or *those*.**

1 This is my new pen.

2 ________ are my new CDs.

3 ________'s my classroom.

4 ________ are my books.

☆☆ **6 Complete the dialogues with *this*, *that*, *these* or *those* and the names of the objects.**

1 **A** What's [1] that ?
B It's my [2] ________ .

2 **A** And what are [3] ________ ?
B They're my [4] ________ .

3 **A** What's [5] ________ ?
B It's a [6] ________ .

4 **A** What are [7] ________ ?
B They're my [8] ________ .

F Your Photos

Vocabulary: Appearance

1 Complete the descriptions.

1 Andy is *big* but Sue is ________ .

2 Barbara is ________ but Eddie is ________ .

3 Bob is ________ but Emma is ________ .

4 Joe is ________ but Jim is ________ .

5 Carol is ________ but David is ________ .

2 Correct five mistakes.

This is a photo of my ~~sister~~ brother. He's short and fat, and he's blond. He's in the kitchen. He's the captain of the school basketball team.

Your Turn

3 Complete the sentences with true information. Use the words from Exercise 1.

1 I ________________ .
2 My friend ________________ .
3 My mum ________________ .
4 My teacher ________________ .

Grammar: Articles

Grammar Reference, page 89

☆ **4 Choose the correct words.**

1 My dad is (*a*) / *the* teacher.
2 My grandfather is *a* / *an* old man.
3 Nicola is *a* / *the* captain of the basketball team.
4 Don't write on *a* / *the* board, please.
5 Helen is *a* / *an* tall girl.
6 This is *a* / *an* American magazine.
7 This is *a* / *an* photo of my school.
8 My friends are in *an* / *the* park next to our school.
9 She's *a* / *an* Australian singer.

☆☆ **5 Complete the description of the photo with *a*, *an* or *the*.**

This is [1] *a* photo of my family. In [2] ________ photo we are in front of our house. It's [3] ________ old house with [4] ________ garden. [5] ________ garden is behind the house. My cousin is in [6] ________ photo with us – she's [7] ________ tall girl next to me. She's [8] ________ student now. Our dog is in [9] ________ photo, too.

6 Write sentences.

Sentence Builder

1 she / girl / short / in my class
She's a short girl in my class.
2 this / computer / new / from Japan
____
3 Miss Brown / teacher / old / at my school
____
4 she / student / Australian / from Sydney
____
5 he / basketball player / great / from New York
____

Module 1 The Challenge

Get Ready

Vocabulary: Interests

1 Look at the pictures and write the names of the interests.

1 *chess*

2 c__________

3 c__________

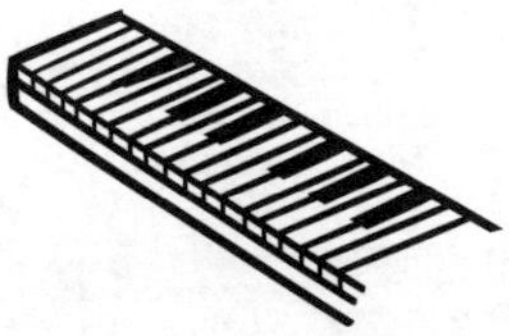

4 m__________

5 p__________

6 f__________

7 r__________

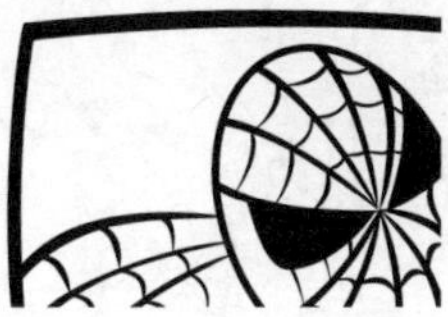

8 f__________

Listening

02 **2** Listen and complete the forms.

FACE Activity Programme

Name	*Angela Lazzeri*
Age	1________
From	*Milan in* 2________
Interests	3________ *and music*

FACE Activity Programme

Name	*Ben* 4________
Age	*thirteen*
From	*Kyoto in* 5________
Interests	*Computers and* 6________

FACE Activity Programme

Name	*Susannah* 7________
Age	8________
From	*York*
Interests	9________, *horse riding and* 10________

02 **3** Listen again. Match the sentences (a–e) to the people (1–3).

1 Angela [*c*] [ ]
2 Ben [ ] [ ]
3 Susannah [ ]

a My mum is English.
b Computers are fantastic.
c We're in York for a year.
d My dad is English.
e My favourite thing is horse riding.

Your Turn

4 Complete the form with true information.

FACE Activity Programme

Name	
Age	
From	
Interests	

5 Who has the same interests as you: Angela, Ben or Susannah?

1 Vocabulary and Grammar

Vocabulary: Abilities

1 **Find twelve abilities in the word snake and label the pictures.**

1 *act* ________

2 ________

3 ________

4 ________

5 ________

writestoriesplayamusicalinstrumentrideabikesinguseacomputertakephotosspeakChinesedrawplaychessactcookpaint

6 ________

7 ________

8 ________

9 ________

10 ________

11 ________

12 ________

Grammar: *can* (ability)

➤ Grammar Reference, page 90

Your Turn

☆ **2** **Write your abilities in the correct list. Use the words from Exercise 1.**

I can ...

I can't ...

☆ **3** **Complete the sentences. Use *can* or *can't*.**

1 They *can't act* ________ .

2 They ________ ________ .

3 She ________ ________ .

4 They ________ ________ .

5 He ________ ________ .

6 She ________ ________ .

☆ **4 Match the descriptions to the photos.**

a Gwyneth Paltrow

b Beyoncé

c Jennifer Lopez

1. She can sing and she can dance. Her husband can sing, too. He's an American rapper.
2. She can act and she can sing. She can speak English and Spanish.
3. She can act and she can sing a little. Her husband can play the piano and the guitar. He's in a British band.

03 ☆☆ **5 Listen and complete the table with ✓ (*can*) or ✗ (*can't*).**

	Andy	Josh	Emma
write stories		✓	
act			
play the guitar			
sing			
draw			
paint			
take photos			
play chess			
play a musical instrument			

☆☆ **6 Complete the dialogue with *can* or *can't*.**

Josh Hi, this is the 'Act Now' Theatre Group. I'm Josh. I [1] *can* write stories and I [2] ________ act, but I [3] ________ sing. What about you, Andy? [4] ________ you sing?

Andy Yes, I [5] ________, and I [6] ________ play the guitar. Here's a CD of my music group at school.

Josh Fantastic, thanks. And you Emma, what [7] ________ you do?

Emma Well, I [8] ________ play the guitar, but I [9] ________ paint and I [10] ________ draw. I [11] ________ also take photos.

7 Join the sentences with *and* or *but*.

Sentence Builder

1. Josh can write stories. He can act.
   Josh can write stories and he can act.
2. Emma can't play chess. She can draw.
   Emma can't play chess but she can draw.
3. Andy can't play the piano. He can play the guitar.
   ____
4. I can't cook. I can't use a computer.
   ____
5. You can sing. You can act.
   ____
6. We can speak Spanish. We can't speak Italian.
   ____

Your Turn

8 Complete the sentences with true information.

My dad can *take photos* but he can't *draw.*

1. I can ________ and I can ________ .
2. I can ________ but I can't ________ .
3. My friend can ________ and can ________ .
4. My teacher can ________ but ________ can't ________ .
5. My mum can ________ and she can ________ .
6. My cousin can ________ and ________ can ________ .

2 Vocabulary and Grammar

Vocabulary: Verbs + nouns

1 Complete the word map with the words in the box.

Word Builder

~~Chinese~~ ~~chess~~ photos the piano the Internet tennis a computer Spanish a motorbike computer games a horse social networking sites the guitar a blog English a bike stories football a mobile phone emails

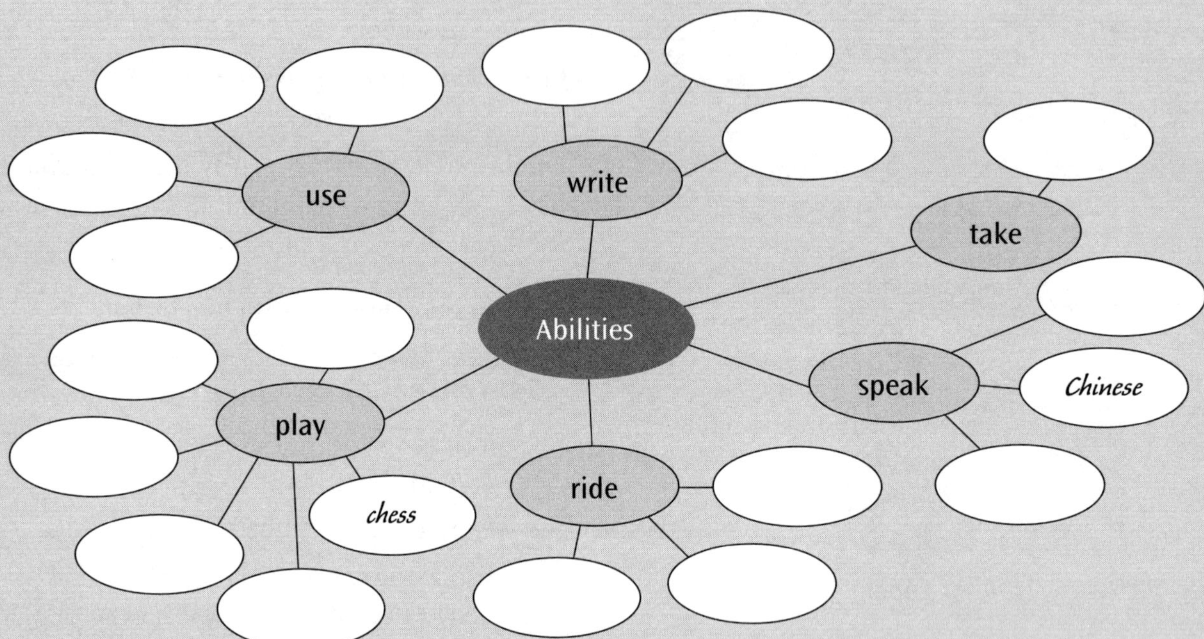

2 Complete the letter.

Dear Kim,

Thanks for your letter. What are my interests? Well, my favourite things are art and music. I can  1 ***draw*** *and*  2 ________. *My mum is a music teacher. She can*  3 ________ *and she can*  4 ________. *My sister and I can*  5 ________.

I'm not very good at sports. I can't  6 ________ *or*  7 ________. *But I can do other practical things. I can*  8 ________ *and I can*  9 ________.

Please write and tell me about your family.

Best wishes,

Jamie

Grammar: Question words

➤ Grammar Reference, page 90

☆ **3 Choose the correct words.**

1 *Who* / *What* is your name?
2 *Where* / *What* are you from?
3 How *many* / *old* are you?
4 *Where* / *What* can you do?
5 *Who* / *What* is your monitor?
6 How *old* / *many* instruments can you play?

☆ **4 Match the questions in Exercise 3 to these answers.**

1 d 2 ☐ 3 ☐ 4 ☐ 5 ☐ 6 ☐

a Two. The guitar and the piano.
b I'm from York.
c I can play chess.
d Jane Baker.
e I'm thirteen.
f Her name's Mel.

Your Turn

☆☆ **5 Complete the sentences using the words in the box. Then write true answers.**

How old	How many	Where	What	Who

1 *How old* is your best friend?
______
2 ______ students are in your English class?
______
3 ______ can Ana Ivanovic do?
______
4 ______ can paint in your family ?
______
5 ______ is Ben Stiller from?
______
6 ______ is the name of your school?
______
7 ______ is your favourite singer?
______
8 ______ teachers are in your school?
______

☆☆ **6 Complete the interview with your answers.**

Mel Hello. My name's Mel. I'm a monitor on the FACE activity programme. What's your name?
You 1 ______
Mel And how old are you?
You 2 ______
Mel Where are you from?
You 3 ______
Mel Where is that?
You 4 ______
Mel Okay, what's your favourite school subject?
You 5 ______
Mel And what are your interests?
You 6 ______
Mel And what can you do?
You 7 ______
Mel Thank you.
You That's okay.

☆ **7 What am I?**

I can't sing but you can listen to music on me.
I can't take photos but you can look at photos on me.
I can't watch films but you can watch DVDs on me.
I can't write but you can write e-mails on me.
I'm a _ _ _ _ _ _ _ _ _ _.

3 Skills

Vocabulary: Opinion adjectives

1 Find nine more opinion adjectives in the word square.

I	Y	U	V	B	M	N	B	X	W	B	X
N	X	O	Z	D	B	P	O	K	I	R	G
T	Z	K	G	U	D	S	R	I	E	I	R
E	B	A	K	N	C	N	I	P	N	L	E
R	C	Y	W	O	M	S	N	N	M	L	A
E	W	Z	A	T	S	I	G	B	C	I	T
S	G	S	L	B	F	O	P	S	O	A	F
T	J	F	Q	A	N	B	T	I	R	N	C
I	I	L	H	D	I	Q	R	L	K	T	O
N	L	Y	R	E	C	H	F	L	M	X	O
G	T	R	P	R	E	T	T	Y	N	Z	L

3 Complete the sentences with true information.

1 I'm into ______________ .
2 I'm mad about ______________ .
3 I'm not very interested in ______________ .
4 ______________ is boring.
5 ______________ is nice.
6 ______________ is cool.
7 ______________ is brilliant.
8 My friend is into ______________ .
9 Our teacher is interested in ______________ .

Key Expressions: Opinions

2 Complete the conversations. Choose a, b or c.

a Yes, I am.
(b) Yes, I can.
c Yes, it is.

---

1 What are you into?
a Yes, I am.
b It's okay.
c Computers. They're great.

2 Are you interested in animals?
a Yes, it's nice.
b Yes, he's interesting.
c No, I'm not.

3 I'm into dance. And you?
a Yes, it's cool.
b Yes, it is.
c No, he isn't.

4 Is your teacher nice?
a Yes, he is.
b Yes, it's interesting.
c No, it isn't.

5 Are you into computers?
a Yes, I'm mad about them.
b Yes, it's fantastic.
c No, it's boring.

Listening

04 **4 Listen and match the interests (a–h) to the people (1–6).**

1 Leo *e*
2 Helen ☐
3 David ☐
4 Rani ☐
5 Sarah ☐
6 James ☐

a photography
b computers
c tennis
d fashion
e music
f films
g art
h animals

Reading

5 Look at the form. Are the sentences true (✓) or false (✗)?

www.onlinesign-up.org/form

First name:	Rachel
Surname:	Hadding
Age:	15
Nationality:	American
City/Town:	Miami
School:	Lake City High School
Teacher:	Mrs King
Skills:	play the guitar, paint and draw, use a computer
Interests:	music, art, computers

1 Rachel is from the United States. ✓
2 Rachel is fifteen. ☐
3 Her teacher is Mrs Lake. ☐
4 Rachel can play the guitar but she can't use a computer. ☐
5 Rachel is into music. ☐
6 Rachel isn't interested in art. ☐

Writing

6 Correct six mistakes.

www.onlinesign-up.org/form

First name:	John ~~Ellis~~
Surname:	*Ellis*
Age:	therteen
Nationality:	Australia
City/Town:	Melbourne
School:	Mr Williams
Teacher:	Lake City High School
Skills:	films, fashion
Interests:	use a computer, ride a bicycle

7 Complete the form with information about Sam.

My name's Sam Harper. I'm fourteen years old and I'm from Toronto in Canada. My school is called Fairfield High School. My teacher is Mr Andrews. I can ride a horse and I can play chess. I can also use a computer. I'm into music and films. I'm also interested in photography.

www.onlinesign-up.org/form

First name:	
Surname:	
Age:	
Nationality:	
City/Town:	
School:	
Teacher:	
Skills:	
Interests:	

Language Check 1

Vocabulary

1 Put the letters in order to make interests.

yetpotr — p*ottery*

1 agohyptporh — p__________
2 snetni — t__________
3 iumcs — m__________
4 sehse — c__________
5 giyelcn — c__________
6 sifml — f__________
7 soreh ngiird — h__________ r__________
8 nfhaios — f__________
9 stoeprmue — c__________

☐ / 9

2 Cross out the wrong words.

I can't ride a bicycle / ~~a map~~ / a horse / a motorbike.

1 I can play tennis / chess / computers / the guitar.
2 Please write a story / the Internet / an email / a blog.
3 We can speak China / Spanish / Italian / Japanese.
4 Can you use social networking sites / computer games / a mobile phone / a computer?
5 History is okay / interesting / great / pretty.
6 I'm into rap. It's cool / great / not bad / boring.

☐ / 6

Grammar

3 Complete the sentences with *can* or *can't*.

What can *you do? I* can *sing and dance.*

1 I'm into languages. I __________ speak German and Russian.
2 We can write stories but we __________ act.
3 '__________ you draw?' 'Yes, I can.'
4 '__________ your brother play chess?' 'No, he can't.'
5 'Can Tania ride a motorbike?' 'No, she __________.'
6 I'm interested in cycling classes – I __________ ride a bike.
7 I'm not into music. I __________ sing or play the guitar.
8 Simon __________ draw and he can paint.

☐ / 8

4 Complete the questions with question words.

'Who*'s your best friend?' 'My best friend is Claire.'*

1 '__________ old are you?'
'I'm thirteen.'
2 '__________ people are at your youth club?'
'Forty.'
3 '__________'s your surname?'
'Davies.'
4 '__________ can speak Italian?'
'My dad can.'
5 '__________ are they from?'
'They're from Rome.'
6 '__________'s the name of your school?'
'City High School.'
7 '__________ languages can you speak?'
'Two. Spanish and German.'

☐ / 7

Key Expressions

5 Choose the correct words.

A This programme is *pretty* / (*great*). What [1]*can* / *are* you interested [2]*in* / *into*?
B I'm mad [3]*about* / *into* music. It's really [4]*cool* / *boring*. [5]*Am* / *Are* you into music too?
A Yes, I am.

☐ / 5

What's your score?

Module 1

☐ Vocabulary
☐ Grammar
☐ Key Expressions
☐ / 35

This is easy.
I need more practice.
This is difficult.

Module 2 Exercise

Get Ready

Vocabulary: Sport and exercise

1 **Complete the puzzle. What's the mystery sport?**

2 **Write the words from Exercise 1 in the correct list.**

do	play	—
________	*rugby*	________
________	________	________
________	________	________
	________	________
		________

Listening

05 **3** **Listen and write the correct sport.**

1 *tennis* 2 ________
3 ________ 4 ________
5 ________ 6 ________

06 **4** **Who's Kelly? Listen and tick the correct picture.**

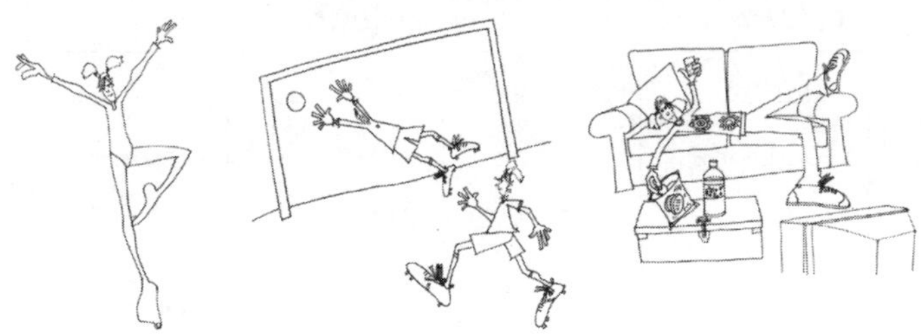

a ☐ **b** ☐ **c** ☐

Your Turn

5 **Complete the sentences about sports and exercise with true information.**

1 I can do ________ . I can't play ________ .

2 I'm into ________ and ________ .

3 ________ is boring but ________ is great.

4 Vocabulary and Grammar

Vocabulary: Appearance and clothes

1 Write the names of the clothes.

Richard:

______ ______ ______ ______

______ ______ ______ ______

Rachel:

______ ______ ______

______ ______ ______

2 Write the words under the correct headings.

~~black~~ short fair earring long blue curly blond ponytail brown dark green shaved head red straight tattoo

hair colour	hairstyle	eye colour	other
black	______	______	______
______	______	______	______
______	______	______	
______	______		
______	______		
	______		

3 Match words from A and B. Are they one or two words?

Word Builder

A ~~book~~ sports hair ear tennis track fashion computer pony

B ring star player tail style ~~shelf~~ game magazine suit

1 *bookshelf*
2 ______
3 ______
4 ______
5 ______
6 ______
7 ______
8 ______
9 ______

Grammar: *have got/has got*

➤ Grammar Reference, page 91

☆ **4 Write pairs of sentences.**

1 he / a ponytail; he / a shaved head
He hasn't got a ponytail. He's got a shaved head.

2 she / blond hair; she / a long dark ponytail

____

3 he / long hair; he / short dark hair

____

4 he / a shaved head; he / long curly hair

____

5 they / blond hair; they / long dark hair

____

☆ **5 Match the descriptions in Exercise 4 to the photos.**

1 ☐ 2 ☐ 3 ☐ 4 ☐ 5 ☐

a

b

c

d

e

☆☆ **6 Choose the correct words. Then choose the correct name.**

One of my favourite sports stars ¹(*is*) / *has* from Argentina. He ²*has* / *'s* in the Barcelona and Argentinian teams. He ³*'s* / *has* about 30 years old. He ⁴*hasn't* / *isn't* very tall but he's slim and he ⁵*'s* / *is* got brown eyes. He ⁶*hasn't* / *haven't* got very long hair. He ⁷*hasn't* / *isn't* married but he ⁸*'s* / *'ve* got a girlfriend. He ⁹*is* / *'s* got two brothers and a sister. He ¹⁰*'s* / *is* also got two cousins called Maxi and Emanuel. They ¹¹*'re* / *'ve* into football, too.

He is **a** Zlatan Ibrahimovic
b Lionel Messi
c Fernando Torres

Your Turn

☆☆ **7 Write questions and true answers.**

have / eyes / colour / what / got / you
What colour eyes have you got?
I've got blue eyes.

1 blond / got / you / have / hair

____

____

2 dark / got / your / has / hair / teacher

____

____

3 got / mother / ponytail / has / your / a

____

____

4 got / you / a / have / tattoo

____

____

5 have / parents / colour / what / got / eyes / your

____

____

6 got / what / you / have / hairstyle

____

____

8 Join the sentences.

Sentence Builder

1 I've got blue eyes. I've got dark hair.
I've got blue eyes and dark hair.

2 You are short. You are slim.

____

3 My cousin is tall. My cousin is pretty.

____

4 My mother has got dark hair. My mother has got brown eyes.

____

5 We have got blue eyes. We have got blond hair.

____

5 Vocabulary and Grammar

Vocabulary: Food and drink

1 Complete the descriptions.

1 I've got some [1] *chicken* and [2] ________ .
I've got an [3] ________ and an [4] ________ .
I've also got a litre of [5] ________ .

2 I've got some [6] ________ with [7] ________ .
I've got some [8] ________ and some [9] ________ .
I've also got a litre of [10] ________ .

2 Find the odd one out.

1	apples	(beans)	oranges
2	chicken	milk	tea
3	salad	vegetables	fish
4	biscuits	crisps	nuts
5	tea	cola	coffee

3 Write four examples from Exercise 2 in the lists.

☺	☹
________	________
________	________
________	________
________	________

Grammar: Countable/uncountable nouns, *some* and *any*

➤ Grammar Reference, page 91

☆ **4 Write the names of the food and drinks under the correct headings.**

Countable	Uncountable
biscuits	*water*
________	________
________	________
________	________

☆☆ **5 Circle the countable noun and underline the uncountable noun in each sentence.**

1. I've got dark hair and blue eyes.
2. Eat some fruit and vegetables.
3. Here's a glass of milk for you.
4. I haven't got any money for sweets.
5. Put some cheese on your pizza.
6. I've got some fish and a salad for lunch.
7. I'm into music. I can play the guitar.
8. We've got four exercises for homework.

☆ **6 Choose the correct words.**

1. Have an / *any* apple for dessert.
2. Eat three *meal / meals* a day.
3. We've got *some / any* coffee but we haven't got *some / any* tea.
4. Have we got *any / some* cola?
5. I can cook *a / some* pasta for you.
6. I've got *a / some* sandwiches for lunch.
7. Don't eat *some / any* ice cream before dinner.
8. Have you got *a / any* money with you?

☆☆ **7 Complete the note. Choose the correct answers, a, b, or c.**

Hi Millie
I'm at grandma's house. It's her birthday today. Please go to the shops after school. Buy [1]________ big cake and [2]________ ice cream. I've got [3]________ presents for grandma but please choose [4]________ birthday card for her. And don't forget to buy [5]________ flowers. You can take [6]________ money from my purse.
Thanks very much.
See you later.
Mum

1	**a** an	**b** a	**c** some
2	**a** some	**b** a	**c** any
3	**a** an	**b** any	**c** some
4	**a** an	**b** some	**c** a
5	**a** some	**b** any	**c** a
6	**a** a	**b** some	**c** any

☆☆ **8 Complete the dialogue with the words in the box.**

any (x 2) a (x 2) ~~two~~ an some (x 3)

A What have you got for lunch?
B [1] *Two* cheese sandwiches and [2]________ apple. Boring!
A Have you got [3]________ water or orange juice?
B No, I haven't.
A Here, have [4]________ of my orange juice.
B Oh, great, thanks. What have you got for lunch?
A [5]________ rice with chicken, and [6]________ fruit salad.
B Very healthy!
A Mmm, my dad is into healthy food – I haven't got [7]________ biscuits or sweets today.
B So, what's your favourite meal?
A Pizza, with [8]________ very big bottle of cola, then [9]________ chocolate ice cream.
B Brilliant!

Your Turn

☆☆☆ **9 Write about your favourite food.**

Favourite meal on your birthday:
a big pizza and some ice cream

- Favourite lunch on a school day:
____
- Favourite food before exercise:
____
- Favourite family meal:
____
- Favourite meal on your birthday:
____

6 Skills

Key Expressions: Asking how things are

1 Cross out the wrong answers.

1 **A** How are things?
B Great. / Not too bad. / ~~It's hard work~~.

2 **A** How is the new youth club?
B It's fantastic. / It's easy. / It's not bad.

3 **A** How are your guitar classes?
B They're difficult. / It's difficult. / They're not bad.

4 **A** How is your photography class going?
B It's okay. / It's great. / She's funny.

5 **A** How are your judo classes?
B They're hard work. / They're horrible. / I'm really hot.

Listening

07 **2 Listen to Linda talking to Tim about how things are. Tick the correct answer.**

1	Linda is	**a** happy.	☐
		b sad.	☐
		c tired.	✓
2	Which classes is Linda in at the youth club?	**a** judo and running	☐
		b gymnastics and running	☐
		c judo and gymnastics	☐
3	Linda's exercise is	**a** nine hours a week.	☐
		b ninety minutes a day.	☐
		c nine minutes a day.	☐
4	What's Tim's opinion of his new school?	**a** It's great	☐
		b It's horrible.	☐
		c It's boring.	☐
5	Tim has got a match on	**a** Sunday.	☐
		b Monday.	☐
		c Saturday.	☐
6	Linda's advice is to	**a** drink fruit juice.	☐
		b eat fruit.	☐
		c drink water.	☐

Your Turn

3 **Complete the dialogue.**

Your friend Hi! How are things?

You ____________________

Your friend How is your exercise class going?

You ____________________

Your friend How are your maths lessons?

You ____________________

Your friend And how are your computer classes?

You ____________________

Reading

4 **Match the words (a–j) to the symbols (1–10).**

1	c	e	**a**	are you
2	ur		**b**	later
3	TB		**c**	today
4	pls		**d**	your
5	r u		**e**	see
6	2		**f**	very
7	gr8		**g**	text me back
8	v		**h**	please
9	2day		**i**	to
10	l8r		**j**	great

5 **Match the answers (a–e) to the text messages (1–5).**

1 d **2** ☐ **3** ☐ **4** ☐ **5** ☐

1. Hi! R U OK?
2. ur piano class OK?
3. Hi! film is on at 5
4. Where R U 2day?
5. How r ur classes?

a OK. C U at cinema.
b No, v hard.
c Judo ☺. Piano ☹.
d Gr8 thanx.
e at sports club.

6 **Write the text message in complete sentences.**

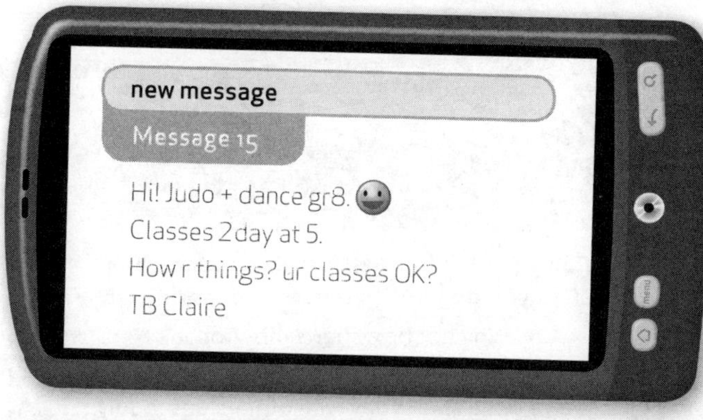

7 **Read the message and choose the correct words.**

1. The text is *to* / *from* Claire.
2. Claire is *happy* / *sad*.
3. Claire *is* / *isn't* into exercise.
4. She *has* / *hasn't* got classes today.
5. Her classes are at *two* / *five* o'clock.

Writing

8 **Text Claire back.**

- Say how things are.
- Give information about good classes.
- Give information about bad lessons.

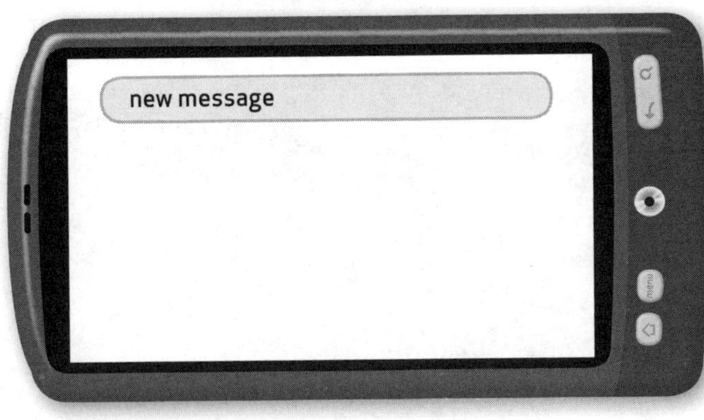

Reading Corner 1

Who is Jeremy King?

1 Read the text. Choose the correct answers.

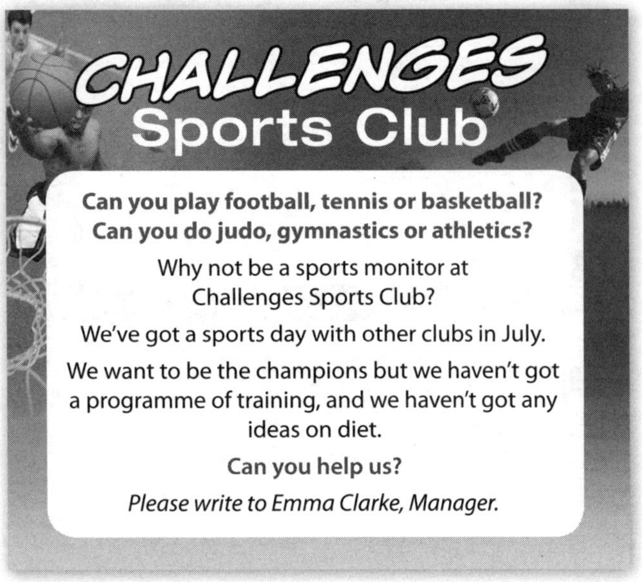

1 The text is an advert for
 a a sports club.
 b a job.
 c a sports day.

2 Challenges Sports Club is interested in
 a a manager.
 b a footballer.
 c a sports monitor.

3 Emma Clarke wants help with
 a training and diet.
 b a sports day.
 c judo classes.

2 Read the letter. Match (a–d) to (1–4) .

47 Dover Street
Highgate
London
N330

April 2011

Dear Miss Clarke,

My name is Jeremy King. I'm twenty-eight years old and I'm from Highgate in London. I am interested in the job of sports monitor at the Challenges Sports Club.

I'm really into sports and exercise. I can play football, tennis and basketball. I can also do judo and athletics. I've got a gold medal in the men's 10,000 metres and I've also got a silver medal in judo.

I've got a brilliant programme for training and diet. It's got advice from food experts and lots of interesting ideas for training. My programme is top secret – only I can help your students to be sports champions.

My email address is jking@mail.com. Please send me a message if you are interested in meeting.

Best wishes,

Jeremy King

Jeremy King

1 Jeremy is ☐
2 Jeremy can ☐
3 Jeremy wants ☐
4 Jeremy has got ☐

a do judo.
b into different sports.
c a secret training programme.
d to help Challenges Sports Club.

3 **Read the information and dialogues 1–3. Who is the real Jeremy King?**

Emma Clarke wants to meet Jeremy King but three men are at the Challenges Sports Club. They all say that *they* are Jeremy!

Dialogue 1

Emma Hello, I'm Emma Clarke.
Jeremy 1 My name's Jeremy King. Nice to meet you.
Emma Where are you from?
Jeremy 1 I'm from Highgate in London.
Emma And how old are you?
Jeremy 1 I'm 28 years old.
Emma Can you do judo?
Jeremy 1 Yes, I can. I've got a silver medal in judo.
Emma How many medals have you got?
Jeremy 1 I've got two medals. I've got a gold medal in the men's 1,000 metres.
Emma What sports can you play?
Jeremy 1 I can play football and basketball.
Emma What advice can you give us about diet?
Jeremy 1 Sorry, I can't give you any advice about food.

1

Dialogue 2

Emma Hello, I'm Emma Clarke.
Jeremy 2 My name's Jeremy King. Nice to meet you.
Emma Where are you from?
Jeremy 2 I'm from Highgate in London.
Emma And how old are you?
Jeremy 2 I'm 26 years old.
Emma What advice can you give us about diet?
Jeremy 2 Eat lots of steak and potatoes but don't eat fruit.
Emma What sports can you play?
Jeremy 2 I can play football and tennis.
Emma How many medals have you got?
Jeremy 2 I've got a gold medal in the men's 10,000 metres.
Emma And can you do judo?
Jeremy 2 No, I can't.

2

Dialogue 3

Emma Hello, I'm Emma Clarke.
Jeremy 3 My name's Jeremy King. Nice to meet you.
Emma Where are you from?
Jeremy 3 I'm from Highgate in London.
Emma And how old are you?
Jeremy 3 I'm 28 years old.
Emma What advice can you give us about diet?
Jeremy 3 Don't eat a lot of steak but eat fish and chicken. Drink lots of water, and eat fruit and nuts.
Emma What sports can you play?
Jeremy 3 I can play basketball, football and tennis.
Emma And can you do judo?
Jeremy 3 Yes, I can. I've got a silver medal in judo.
Emma How many medals have you got?
Jeremy 3 I've got two medals. I've also got a gold medal in the men's 10,000 metres.

3

The real Jeremy King is ________ .

4 **Imagine you are Jeremy King. Write advice for the Challenges Sports Club.**

- ________
- ________
- ________
- Don't ________
- Don't ________
- Don't ________

Language Check 2

Vocabulary

1 Choose the correct words.

I can (run) / dance *the 100 metres.*

1 I can't *do / play* basketball.
2 Can you *do / play* athletics?
3 I can *do / play* tennis.
4 *Do / Play* exercise every day.
5 Don't *play / do* football in the house.
6 Can you *swimming / swim*?
7 Fruit is important. Eat *apples / beans* every day.
8 Have some *milk / cola* in your coffee.
9 I've got an apple and an *biscuit / orange*.
10 Have some *vegetables / crisps* with your fish.

☐ / 10

2 Complete the description.

She's *tall* and [1] ______ . She's got dark [2] ______ and she's got a [3] ______ . She's got a shirt, [4] ______ and [5] ______ .

☐ / 5

Grammar

3 Complete the sentences with the correct form of *have got*.

My team has got *some good players.*

1 I've got a brother but I ______ a sister.
2 What colour eyes ______ you ______ ?
3 My sister ______ blond hair.
4 My classroom ______ a computer but it's got a DVD player.
5 We ______ a new player in our team.
6 ______ your parents ______ dark hair?
7 How many brothers ______ you ______ ?
8 I ______ any tattoos – they're horrible.

☐ / 8

4 Correct the underlined mistakes.

Here is some glass of water for you. *a*

1 Have we got some ice cream? ______
2 Have any of my pizza. It's great. ______
3 I haven't got some homework. ______
4 Don't eat a crisps before lunch. ______
5 Drink some waters. ______
6 They've got a great clothes in that shop. ______
7 We haven't got some biscuits. ______

☐ / 7

Key Expressions

5 Choose the correct words.

A (*How*) / *What* are things?
B Not [1]*very / too* bad.
A How [2]*is / are* your judo class going?
B Horrible! Judo is really [3]*difficult / easy*. I'm really [4]*happy / tired*.
A And how are your Spanish lessons?
B They're [5]*horrible / fantastic*. Spanish is really easy.

☐ / 5

What's your score?

Module 2

☐ Vocabulary
☐ Grammar
☐ Key Expressions
☐ / 35

This is easy.
I need more practice.
This is difficult.

Module 3 Risk

Get Ready

Vocabulary: Jobs

1 **Write the names of the jobs.**

1 *actor*

2 ____________

3 ____________

4 ____________

5 ____________

6 ____________

7 ____________

8 ____________

9 ____________

10 ____________

11 ____________

2 **Match the words (1–4) and (a–d).**

1	fire	**a**	driver
2	police	**b**	cleaner
3	racing	**c**	fighter
4	window	**d**	officer

3 **Find five more adjectives in the word snake. Then write the words in pairs of opposites.**

interestingdangerouseasyboringdifficultsafe

adjective	opposite
interesting	____________
____________	____________
____________	____________

Listening

08 **4** **Listen to four people talk about their jobs. What are they?**

1 *teacher*

2 ____________

3 ____________

4 ____________

Your Turn

5 **What's your opinion? Write adjectives for these jobs.**

racing driver *dangerous, difficult, interesting*

1 vet ____________

2 pilot ____________

3 electrician ____________

4 doctor ____________

5 scientist ____________

7 Vocabulary and Grammar

Vocabulary: Routines

1 Match words from A and B and label the pictures.

A ~~get~~ do brush have play have go have do make watch

B TV cards lunch your homework your teeth ~~up~~ a shower dinner to bed some exercise your bed

a *get up* ☐ **b** ________ ☐ **c** ________ ☐ **d** ________ ☐

e ________ ☐ **f** ________ ☐ **g** ________ ☐ **h** ________ ☐ ________ ☐

i ________ ☐ **j** ________ ☐

2 Number the verbs in Exercise 1 in the order you do them (1 = first).

3 Choose the correct verbs.

1 *do* / (*make*) your bed
2 *wash* / *clean* the floor
3 *do* / *make* the dishes
4 *do* / *make* the housework
5 *clean* / *empty* the rubbish bins
6 *wash* / *do* your clothes
7 *make* / *go* shopping
8 *tidy* / *wash* your room

Grammar: Present Simple (1)

➤ Grammar Reference, page 91–92

☆ **4 Complete the sentences with the correct form of the verbs in the box. Use the Present Simple affirmative.**

do ~~have~~ get up wash go (x2) watch tidy

1 I *have* breakfast at 7.30.
2 Joe ________ his room at weekends.
3 My sister ________ the dishes in the evening.
4 Mum and Dad ________ shopping on Saturdays.
5 My friend and I ________ TV after school.
6 My grandma ________ to bed at 10.00.
7 Dad ________ our clothes.
8 You ________ very early.

Grammar: Present Simple (2)

➤ Grammar Reference, page 91–92

☆ **5 Correct the underlined mistakes using negatives.**

1 I <u>not</u> get up at 6.30.
don't

2 Helen <u>don't</u> have lunch at school.
______

3 You <u>no</u> tidy your room.
______

4 We <u>aren't</u> go to school at weekends.
______

5 James doesn't <u>studies</u> music.
______

☆☆ **6 Complete the description with the correct form of the Present Simple. Then guess the job.**

William is a(n) ______ .

My friend William has got an interesting job. He [1] *gets up* (get up) at different times every day. He [2] ______ (not go) to a hospital for his job and he [3] ______ (not work) in a school. He [4] ______ (not have) a uniform in his job. He [5] ______ (do) some exercise every day – it's important for him to be slim. He [6] ______ (not sing) and he [7] ______ (not dance) in his job, but he [8] ______ (learn) a new part every month.

☆☆ **7 Look at the pictures and complete the text. Use the correct form of the Present Simple.**

My name's Liz and Saturday is my favourite day!

I  [1] *don't go to school*. I  [2] ______ at 9.30 and I  [3] ______ . My mum  [4] ______ and then my dad  [5] ______ . My brother and I  [6] ______ . In the afternoon, my family and I  [7] ______ .

Your Turn

☆☆☆ **8 Complete the description of your Saturdays with the verbs in the box.**

get up   have breakfast   go to work   tidy my room   watch TV   go shopping

On Saturdays I ______ at ______ . I ______ with my family. My parents ______ . I ______ and then I ______ . In the afternoon I ______ .

9 Write true sentences about routines.

Sentence Builder

I / *activity*; *day*

I go shopping on Saturdays

1 I / get up; time
______

2 My family and I / *activity*; evening
______

3 My friends and I / *activity*; afternoon
______

4 I / go to bed; *time*
______

5 We / not go to school; *day*
______

6 I / not study; *day*
______

8 Vocabulary and Grammar

Vocabulary: The Internet

1 Complete the verbs with the letters, *a, e, i, o* or *u*.

1 rec *e* *i* ve an email/an attachment
2 ch _ t online
3 d _ wnl _ _ d music/a file/a photo
4 s _ v _ a file / an email/an attachment
5 d _ l _ t _ a file/an email/an attachment
6 _ s _ a password/a nickname

Safe and dangerous activities

2 Match the verbs (1–8) and the words (a–j) to make phrases. Some verbs have two answers.

1	smoke	a	a motorbike
2	use	b	the street
3	go	c	by car
4	ride	d	a mobile phone
5	travel	e	cigarettes
6	wear	f	rugby
7	play	g	by plane
8	cross	h	a helmet
		i	skiing
		j	a bike

3 What do you think is safe or dangerous? Write the activities from Exercise 1.

Safe

____

____

____

____

____

Very Dangerous

4 Replace the underlined words with the expressions in the box.

Sentence Builder

every day ~~every month~~ every week
every weekend every year

1 I see my grandparents 12 times a year.
every month
2 I get up at 8.00 Monday to Sunday.
____
3 We go to the cinema on Saturdays or Sundays. _______________
4 My friend goes to Spain every summer.
____
5 I tidy my room on Wednesdays.
____

Your Turn

5 Write true sentences about your school life. Use the phrases in the box.

check the science equipment
play sport speak English
use a computer walk to school

1 I _______________ .
2 My teacher _______________ .
3 My class _______________ .
4 We _______________ .
5 I _______________ .

Grammar: Present Simple (3)

➤ Grammar Reference, page 91–92

☆ **6 Look at the pictures. Write questions and answers.**

David

Tim and Joe

Sue

Alison and Linda

1 David / ride a bike to school
Does David ride a bike to school ? *Yes, he does.*

2 David / wear a helmet
______________________ ? __________ .

3 Tim and Joe / smoke cigarettes
______________________ ? __________ .

4 Sue / go skateboarding
______________________ ? __________ .

5 Sue / wear safety clothes
______________________ ? __________ .

6 Alison and Linda / play football
______________________ ? __________ .

7 Alison and Linda / play in a safe place
______________________ ? __________ .

☆ **7 Who in Exercise 5 is safe?**

____

☆ **8 Write questions for the answers.**

1 *How do you go to school?*
I go to school by bike.

2 ______________________
I use the Internet for two hours every day.

3 ______________________
My mum works in a hospital.

4 ______________________
My parents go to bed at 11.00.

5 ______________________
We watch DVDs in the evening.

6 ______________________
I download music and photos off the Internet.

☆☆ **9 Complete the questions in the questionnaire. Then write true answers.**

Travel

1 you / wear a helmet / on your bike?
______________________ .

2 how many streets / you / cross / every day?
______________________ .

Technology

3 how / you contact / your friends, by mobile or email?
______________________ .

4 you / give / people your home address on the Internet?
______________________ .

Weekends

5 where / you / play sport, in the street or in the park?
______________________ .

6 what time / you / see your friends in the evening?
______________________ .

9 Skills

Vocabulary: Feelings

1 Label the pictures with the words in the box.

unhappy relaxed excited nervous ~~bored~~ scared

1 *bored*

2 ________

3 ________

4 ________

5 ________

6 ________

Your Turn

2 Describe your feelings.

1 You're in an exam. ________
2 It's your birthday. ________
3 You're at an adventure park. ________
4 It's the weekend. ________
5 You aren't very well. ________
6 You're at the cinema. ________

Key Expressions: Preferences

3 Write the expressions in the correct order.

I don't mind heights.
~~I love music.~~
I hate swimming.
I like Italian food.
I don't like football.

1 *I love music.*
2 ________
3 ________
4 ________
5 ________

Listening

09 **4 Listen and tick the correct answer.**

1 Where are Ben and Jane?

a ☐

b ☐

c ✓

2 What does Eddie want to do?

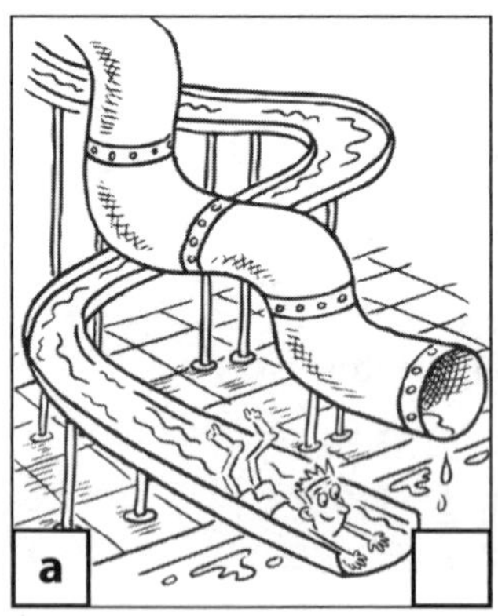

a ☐

b ☐

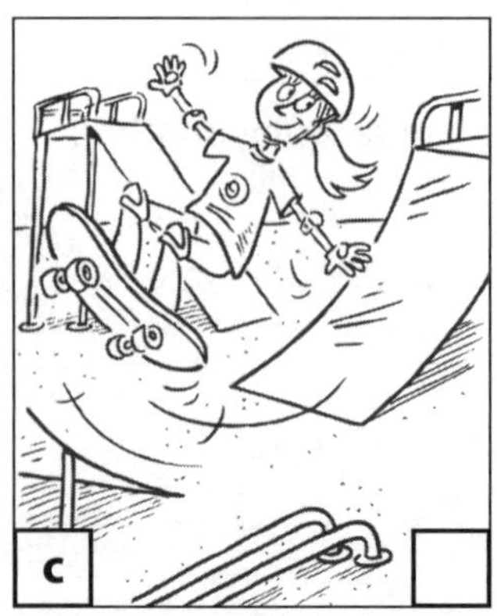

c ☐

3 How does Kelly feel?

nervous	**excited**	**unhappy**
a ☐	b ☐	c ☐

4 What does Adam need to wear?

a ☐

b ☐

c ☐

Your Turn

5 Complete the sentences with true information.

Sentence Builder

1 In my country people love ______________ .
2 I don't mind ______________ .
3 My friends and I don't like ______________ .
4 My mum hates ______________ .
5 I prefer ______________ .

Reading

6 Read the report and answer the questions.

Report: Class 7A
A survey on reading

Ten people in our group love reading. Five people don't mind it and two people hate it.

Eight people like reading sports magazines and six people like music magazines. Three people don't mind reading school books.

Five people read every day. Ten people read every week and twelve people read every weekend. Reading magazines and reading at weekends are popular in our group.

1 How many people don't like reading?
____
2 Which are more popular: sports magazines or music magazines?
____
3 Do some students read school books?
____
4 When is a popular time for reading?
____

Writing

7 Look at the table. Find four mistakes in the first part of the report below.

	love	like	don't like	don't mind	hate
Cooking		2	4		2
Watching films	7	5		1	
Taking photos		6	3		
Playing computer games	10	5			1

Report: Class
A survey on interests

Three people in our group like cook. Four people not like it and two people hate.

8 Complete the report using the information in the table. Use the report in Exercise 6 to help you.

Language Check 3

Vocabulary

1 Write the words under the correct headings.

bored ~~builder~~ electrician excited fire fighter ~~nervous~~ nurse relaxed scared unhappy vet waiter

Jobs	Feelings
builder	*nervous*

/ 10

2 Write the correct verbs.

get up *at eight o'clock*

1 ____________ your teeth
2 ____________ the housework
3 ____________ TV
4 ____________ shopping
5 ____________ a shower

/ 5

Grammar

3 Complete the text with the correct form of the Present Simple.

On Saturdays, my brother and I *get up* (get up) at 8.00. Our cousin, Anna, [1]____________ (get up) at 10.00. I [2]____________ (make) my bed and my brother [3]____________ (tidy) his room. Anna [4]____________ (not do) housework. I [5]____________ (do) athletics and my brother [6]____________ (do) judo. Anna [7]____________ (watch) TV for hours. I think her life is boring!

/ 7

4 Complete the dialogue.

A *Do* you have breakfast every day?
B Yes, I [1]____________ . I have cereal and fruit.
A And [2]____________ you and your friends do exercises?
B No, we [3]____________ .
A [4]____________ many hours do you chat online?
B About two hours.
A [5]____________ time [6]____________ you go to bed?
B At about nine o'clock.
A [7]____________ your brother go to bed at nine o'clock?
B No, he [8]____________ . He goes to bed at eleven o'clock!

/ 8

Key Expressions

5 Complete the sentences with the words in the box.

love hate don't like don't mind like

My new trainers are fantastic. I love *them.*

1 History is interesting. I ____________ it.
2 Football is OK. I ____________ it.
3 Chess is boring. I ____________ it.
4 Dogs are horrible. I ____________ them.
5 English is great. I ____________ it.

/ 5

What's your score?

Module 3

- Vocabulary
- Grammar
- Key Expressions

/ 35

This is easy.
I need more practice.
This is difficult.

Module 4 Out and About

Get Ready

Vocabulary: Places

1 Look at the objects and complete the names of the places they belong in.

1

2

3

4

5

6

7

8

1 *snack bar* ____________
2 ____________
3 ____________
4 ____________
5 ____________
6 ____________
7 ____________
8 ____________

2 Write advice. Use names of places.

1 'I love dancing.' *Go to the under-16s club.*
2 'I'm into films.' ____________
3 'I love swimming.' ____________
4 'I like animals.' ____________
5 'I'm into sport and exercise.' ____________
6 'I'm interested in history.' ____________

Listening

10 **3** Where do they want to go? Match the people with three of the places.

1 Hannah *c*   2 Tom __   3 Sarah __

Your Turn

4 Where do you want to go? Choose places for these situations.

1 It's Saturday afternoon and you're bored.
____
2 It's your birthday. ____________
3 It's Friday evening and the TV is boring.
____
4 It's the last day of term.
____
5 You want to go out with a friend.
____
6 You want to go out in a big group.
____

10 Vocabulary and Grammar

Vocabulary: Free time

1 Write the names of the activities.

hang out at the local park go to the cinema go to the shopping centre play basketball ~~watch DVDs at home~~ spend time with my family ride my bike surf the Internet

1 I watch about three a week on my computer, usually at weekends.
watch DVDs at home ☐

2 I look in the clothes and music shops every weekend.
______ ☐

3 I go about once a month. My favourite actors are Mark Wahlberg and Scarlett Johansson.
______ ☐

4 My friends and I have a match once a week. We train a lot after school.
______ ☐

5 I get information for my homework, or just look for interesting websites.
______ ☐

6 I use it to go to school and a lot at the weekends. It's good exercise.
______ ☐

7 I chat to my mum and dad for an hour every evening after dinner.
______ ☐

8 I go every evening after school. I see my friends there but I don't play on the equipment.
______ ☐

Your Turn

2 Number the activities in Exercise 1 (1 = your favourite activity).

Grammar: Adverbs

➤ Grammar Reference, page 92

☆ **3 Write the words in the correct place in the table.**

~~always~~ never often usually sometimes hardly ever

100% *always*
______
______
______
______
0% ______

☆ **4 Rewrite the sentences using the adverbs in brackets.**

1 We play computer games. (hardly ever)
We hardly ever play computer games.

2 I listen to CDs after school. (always)
______

3 My parents go to the sports centre at weekends. (sometimes)
______

4 You play tennis with me. (never)
______

5 My sister reads in the evening. (usually)
______

6 I go to the skatepark at weekends. (often)
______

11 **5** ☆ **Listen to Tim, Martin and Rachel. Write the correct names under the charts.**

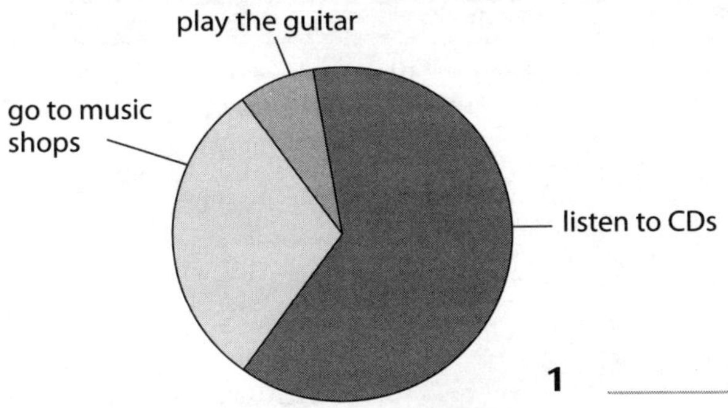

1 ________

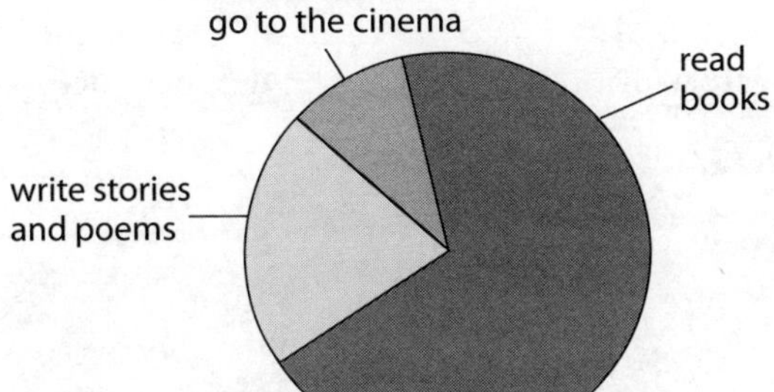

2 ________

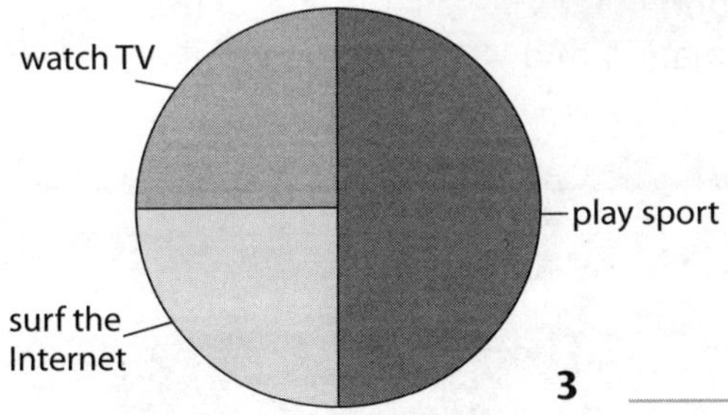

3 ________

☆☆ **6** **Complete the text about the people in Exercise 5 with the pairs of words in the box.**

hardly ever/go sometimes/surf sometimes / write never/read sometimes/go ~~often/play~~ usually/listen hardly ever/play sometimes/watch never/watch usually/read

Rachel [1] *often plays* sport. She [2] ________ TV and she [3] ________ the Internet. She [4] ________ magazines. Tim [5] ________ to CDs or his MP3 player in the evening. He [6] ________ the guitar and he never sings. He [7] ________ to music shops with his friends at the weekends. Martin [8] ________ TV and he never hangs out with people from school. He [9] ________ books in his free time. He [10] ________ stories and poems. He doesn't mind watching DVDs at home, but he [11] ________ to the cinema.

Your Turn

☆☆☆ **7** **Complete the chart for you. Then complete the summary.**

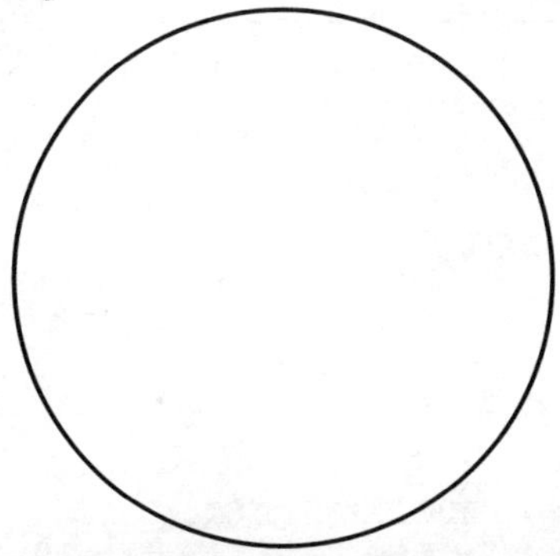

My favourite thing is ________ .
I usually ________ in the evening.
I also like ________ .
I often ________ and I sometimes ________ .
I'm not into ________ .
I don't ________ and I never ________ .

8 **Write the words in the correct order.**

Sentence Builder

1 are / always / late. / You
You are always late.

2 cinema. / go / the / We / hardly ever / to
____

3 bed / goes / John / always / to / late.
____

4 on Saturdays. / at home / never / Dad / is
____

5 happy. / usually / friend / My / is
____

6 at weekends. / bowling alley / I / to / often / go / the
____

11 Vocabulary and Grammar

1 **Match words from A and B to complete the sentences.**

Word Builder

A ~~put~~ sit get find listen talk look

B to out ~~on~~ in to at down

1 *Put on* special glasses and see the film in 3D.

2 ______ about life in the sea at WaterWorld.

3 ______ cars of the future at SpaceRace.

4 ______ spectacular exhibitions of plant life at EcoWorld.

5 ______ the exhibition guides. ______ their information and ask lots of questions.

6 ______ and have a drink in our café.

Grammar: *there is/there are* with *some* and *any*

➤ Grammar Reference, page 92–93

☆ **2** **Complete the descriptions of the places (1–3) with *is*, *are*, *isn't*, *aren't*, *some* or *any*. Then match the photos (a–c) to the descriptions.**

(1) The **Six Flags Great Adventure** is in New Jersey in the United States. There [1] *are* 13 roller coasters in this amusement park – Kingda Ka is about 139 metres high and it's very fast. There [2] ______ also water rides and [3] ______ rides for children. The park has also got a lot of wild animals and there [4] ______ a safari bus tour. ☐

(2) The **Eden Project** is in Cornwall in the south of England. There [5] ______ any rollercoasters or rides here – it is an information centre about plants and the environment. There [6] ______ two special buildings called 'biomes' with thousands of plants from different countries. There aren't [7] ______ real animals but there is a lot of information about animals and plants. ☐

(3) The **National Space Centre** is in Leicester in the centre of England. You can find out about space and other planets. There [8] ______ spectacular exhibitions and interactive activities. There [9] ______ a play area but there are activities for school students and young children. ☐

☆☆ **3 Complete the dialogue with the words in the box.**

there is (x3) are isn't aren't some any (x2)

Ben Hi, Annie. It's Ben here.

Annie Oh, hi Ben. How are things? Do you like your new town?

Ben It's great, thanks. 1 *There* are some cool places to go. There 2 ________ a water park and 3 ________'s an ice rink.

Annie Wow! I love ice skating. And are there 4 ________ skateparks?

Ben No, there 5 ________ . I can't do much skateboarding now.

Annie Oh, that's sad. But what about shopping? How many shopping centres 6 ________ there?

Ben Three. They are all very big and there are 7 ________ good small shops, too.

Annie That's fantastic. There aren't 8 ________ good shops here. 9 ________ there a 3D cinema?

Ben No, there 10 ________ but there 11 ________ a cinema with five screens. We go and see a film there every week.

Annie Cool!

☆☆ **4 Write questions and true short answers about your town.**

good museum?	snack bars?
Is there a good museum?	*Are there any snack bars?*
Yes, there is./ No, there isn't.	*Yes, there are./ No, there aren't.*

1 good music shops?

____

____

2 cinema?

____

____

3 skateparks?

____

____

4 ice rink?

____

____

Your Turn

☆☆☆ **5 Complete the text with true information.**

I live in ________ (name of town). *There* ________ *places for young people. There is* ________ *and there are* ________. *I go to the* ________ (place) *every* ________ (time). *There isn't* ________ *and there aren't* ________. *I think my town is* ________ (interesting/boring).

☆☆☆ **6 Think about your ideal school. Write sentences about five things in the box.**

~~snack bars~~ teachers robots tests sports centre computers books interactive video screens armchairs

1 *There are three snack bars.*

2 ________________________

3 ________________________

4 ________________________

5 ________________________

6 ________________________

Vocabulary: Places

1 Complete the names of the places. Which places are near your school? Tick the boxes.

1 b *a* nk ☐
2 p _ l _ c _ st _ t _ _ n ☐
3 c _ r p _ rk ☐
4 h _ sp _ t _ l ☐
5 p _ st _ ff _ c _ ☐
6 ch _ rch ☐
7 r _ _ lw _ y st _ t _ _ n ☐
8 h _ t _ l ☐
9 t _ _ r _ st _ nf _ rm _ t _ _ n ☐
10 r _ v _ r ☐
11 th _ _ tr _ ☐

2 Look at the map. Complete the directions with the words in the box.

~~opposite~~ cross on the left go past turn right on the right go down turn left on the corner go out of

1 There is a park *opposite* York Minster.
2 ________ the Church onto Parliament Street. ________ into Market Street. The Shambles is ________.
3 There is a bank ________ of Museum Street and Blake Street.
4 ________ Museum Gardens, ________ the river and ________ into North Street and the Hotel is on your right.
5 ________ Coney Street and the bridge over the river is ________.

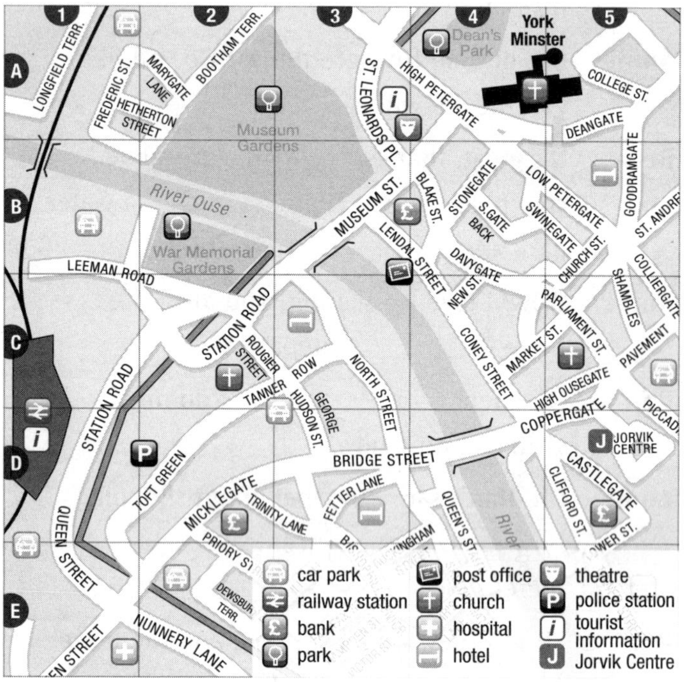

Key Expressions: Asking for and giving directions

3 Complete the dialogue with lines (a–g). There are two lines you don't need.

A Excuse me.
B [1] *e*
A Can you tell me how to get to the post office, please?
B [2] ________
A Oak Street?
B [3] ________
A On the left?
B [4] ________
A Thanks very much.
B [5] ________

a You're welcome.
b That's right. Go down Oak Street, cross Millennium Square and the post office is on the left.
c Go out of the car park and turn right.
d Yes, sure. Go past the police station and turn left into Oak Street.
e ~~Yes?~~
f Yes. You can't miss it. It's opposite the hotel.
g Yes, it's opposite the post office.

Listening

12 **4 Listen to the dialogues and write the names of the places (A, B and C) on the map.**

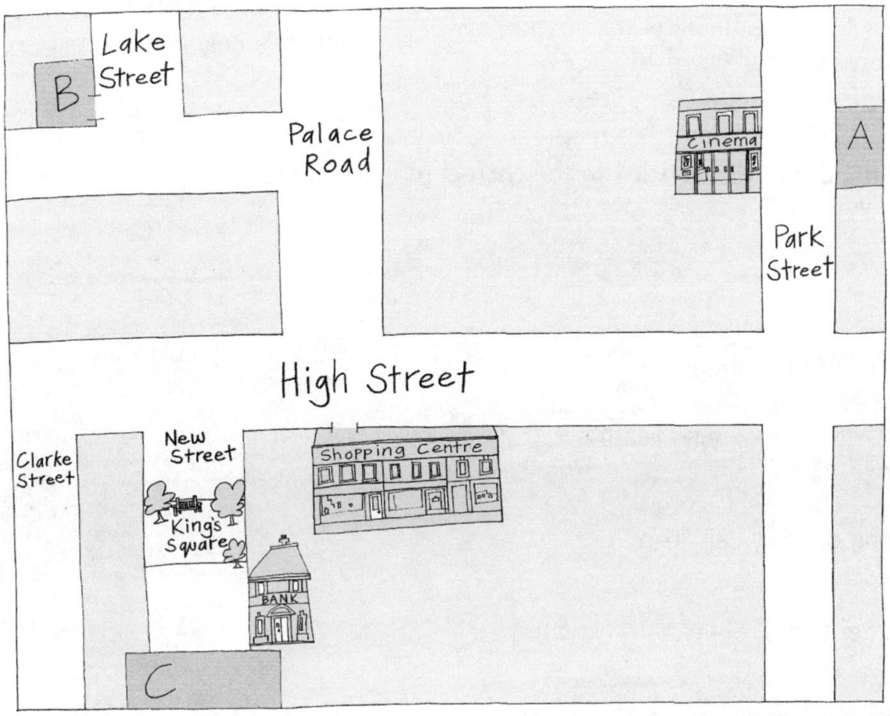

Reading

5 Read the note and choose the correct information.

Hi Simone,
Here are directions to the under-16s club. First, get the bus from your house to the High Street. Stop opposite the shopping centre. Then cross the main road and turn right into Queen Street. Go past the bank on the left and then turn left into White Road. The under-16s club is opposite the ice rink. You can't miss it!
See you at 7.30.
Mark

1 The note is from *Simone* / *Mark*.
2 Simone wants to go to *Mark's house* / *the under-16s club*.
3 Simone *needs* / *doesn't need* to get a bus.
4 Simone needs to *get the bus* / *walk* from the shopping centre.
5 Simone needs to cross *one* / *two* roads.
6 You *can* / *can't* see the ice rink from the under-16s club.

6 Number the directions in the correct order. Then write capital letters where necessary.

Sentence Builder

K S

a go down king street. then cross palace square. ☐
b first, go out of the shopping centre and cross the high street. ☐
c the palace theatre is opposite st mark's church. you can't miss it. ☐
d go down the high street and then turn left into king street. ☐

Writing

7 Write a note to a friend. Give him/her directions from your school to your house. Include *First*, *then*, and *and then*.

Dear ________
Here are directions to my house.

Reading Corner 2

Limericks

1 **Read the definition of *limerick*.**

limerick /ˈlɪmərɪk/ a short, funny poem with five lines, three long and two short

There is a young swimmer called Greg,
Who eats nothing but biscuits and eggs.
He doesn't swim fast,
In races, he's last,
But he's only got very short legs.

2 **Write the missing lines of Limerick 1 in the correct place. Use the rhyme to help you.**

When she walks down the street,

And she often has very cold toes.

Who has got a very long nose.

Limerick 1

There is a young girl they call Rose,

____

She can't see her feet,

____

____

13 **3** **Listen to Limerick 1 and check your answers to Exercise 2.**

4 **Choose the correct words in Limerick 2. Use the rhyme to help you.**

Limerick 2

There *is/has* a young student called *Brett/Brad*,
And *a/an* huge dinosaur *is/are* his pet.
It's *got/has* very sharp *tooth/teeth*,
But it's *every/ever* so sweet,
And it doesn't like seeing the *vet/zoo*.

14 **5** **Listen to Limerick 2 and check your answers to Exercise 4.**

6 **Complete Limerick 3 with the words in the box.**

~~is~~ spends not says crazy in bread young think

Limerick 3

There *is* a ______ student called Daisy.
Her friends all ______ she is ______ .
She ______ all day ______ bed,
Eating chocolate and ______,
And then ______, 'I'm ______ really lazy!'

15 **7** **Listen to Limerick 3 and check your answers to Exercise 6.**

8 **Read Limerick 4 and underline the main stresses on each line.**

Limerick 4

There is a new robot called 'WorkMate',
Who likes doing things that you just hate.
He does homework and tests,
So that you have a rest,
And go out and about with your classmates.

16 **9** **Listen to Limerick 4 and check your answers to Exercise 8.**

10 **Write the lines of Limerick 5 in full. Think about the rhythm to help you.**

Limerick 5

There / young lady / Rome
____

Who / hardly ever / at home
____

She / skateboard / in park
____

And / go swimming / in the dark
____

And / never remember / her comb
____

17 **11** **Listen to Limerick 5 and check your answers to Exercise 10.**

12 **Match the pictures (a–e) to Limericks (1–5). Then read your favourite limerick aloud.**

a ☐

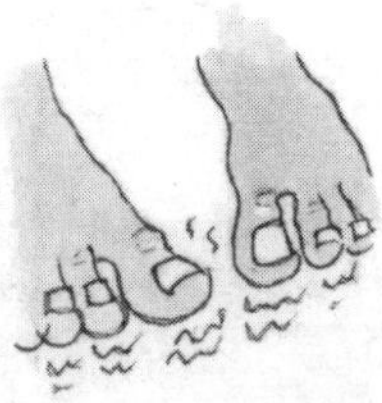
b ☐

c ☐

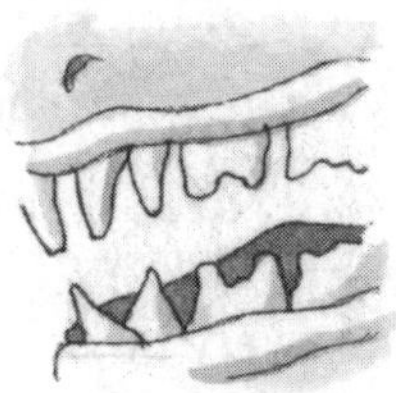
d ☐

e ☐

Language Check 4

Vocabulary

1 Write places for these things.

films – *cinema*

1 emails – I________ c________
2 rides – a________ p________
3 gymnastics – s________ c________
4 trains – r________ s________
5 letters – p________ o________
6 new clothes – s________ c________
7 dancing – u________-16s c________
8 exhibitions – m________
9 money – b________
10 food – s________ b________

☐ / 10

2 Choose the correct words.

I hate getting (up) / down *early.*

1 Don't look *at* / *to* the answers to the exercise.
2 You can find *out* / *up* about different places on the Internet.
3 Sit *out* / *down* and have a drink.
4 I talk *at* / *to* my best friend every day.
5 Can I get *in* / *on* the car now?

☐ / 5

Grammar

3 Reorder the letters in brackets and write the adverbs in the correct place in the sentences.

I play computer games. (adyhrl vere)
I hardly ever play computer games.

1 You arrive late. (nfeot)
____
2 He is happy. (syualul)
____
3 We go to the cinema. (evnre)
____
4 My parents use the Internet. (iosmestme)
____
5 I am at home in the mornings. (aslyaw)
____

☐ / 5

4 Complete the dialogue with *'s*, *isn't*, *are*, *aren't*, *some* or *any*.

Anne Are there [1]________ places for young people in your town?

Joe Yes, there [2]________ . There [3]________ a bowling alley. And there are [4]________ good snack bars.

Anne Wow! There [5]________ any snack bars in my town – it's really small. But there [6]________ an under-16s club at my school.

Joe There [7]________ an under-16s club at my school but there's a good computer club.

Anne How many computers [8]________ there?

Joe About twenty, I think.

Anne Twenty! We haven't got a computer club at my school and there aren't [9]________ Internet cafés in town.

Joe Is there a computer shop?

Anne No, there [10]________ . My town is boring!

☐ / 10

Key expressions

5 Choose the correct words.

A Can you tell me (*how*) / *where* to get to the hospital, please?

B Yes, sure. First, [1]go *down* / *out of* this street and then [2]*turn* / *cross* right opposite the cinema. It's [3]*in* / *on* the corner of the High Street and White Road. Go [4]*past* / *down* the bank on White Road. The hospital is on the left. You can't [5]*miss* / *find* it.

B Thanks very much.

☐ / 5

What's your score?

Module 4

☐ Vocabulary
☐ Grammar
☐ Key Expressions

☐ / 35

This is easy.
I need more practice.
This is difficult.

Module 5 The Weather

Get Ready

Vocabulary: The weather

1 **Find ten weather words. Write them under the correct pictures.**

(rainy)coldcloudyfoggysunnywarmhotwindyicysnowy

1 *rainy*

2 ______

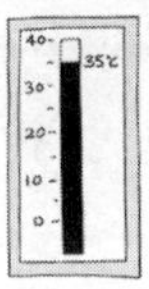

3 ______

4 ______

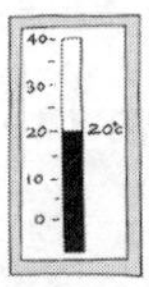

5 ______

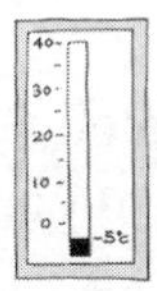

6 ______

7 ______

8 ______

9 ______

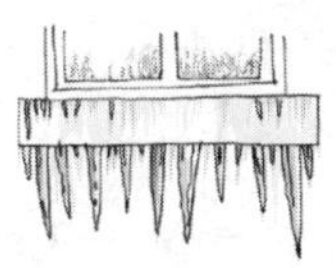

10 ______

2 **Cross out the wrong words.**

1 Look! It's *snowy* / *icy* / ~~warm~~. The street is all white.
2 Great, it's *sunny* / *snowy* / *hot*. We can play tennis.
3 It's very *warm* / *wet* / *sunny*. We can sit in the garden.
4 It's very *foggy* / *sunny* / *snowy*. I can't see the car in front of us.
5 You don't need your boots. It isn't *snowy* / *wet* / *windy* today.
6 Don't forget your jacket. It's *icy* / *wet* / *hot* today.

Listening

18 **3** **What's the weather like in Britain? Listen to three dialogues and copy the correct weather symbols on the map.**

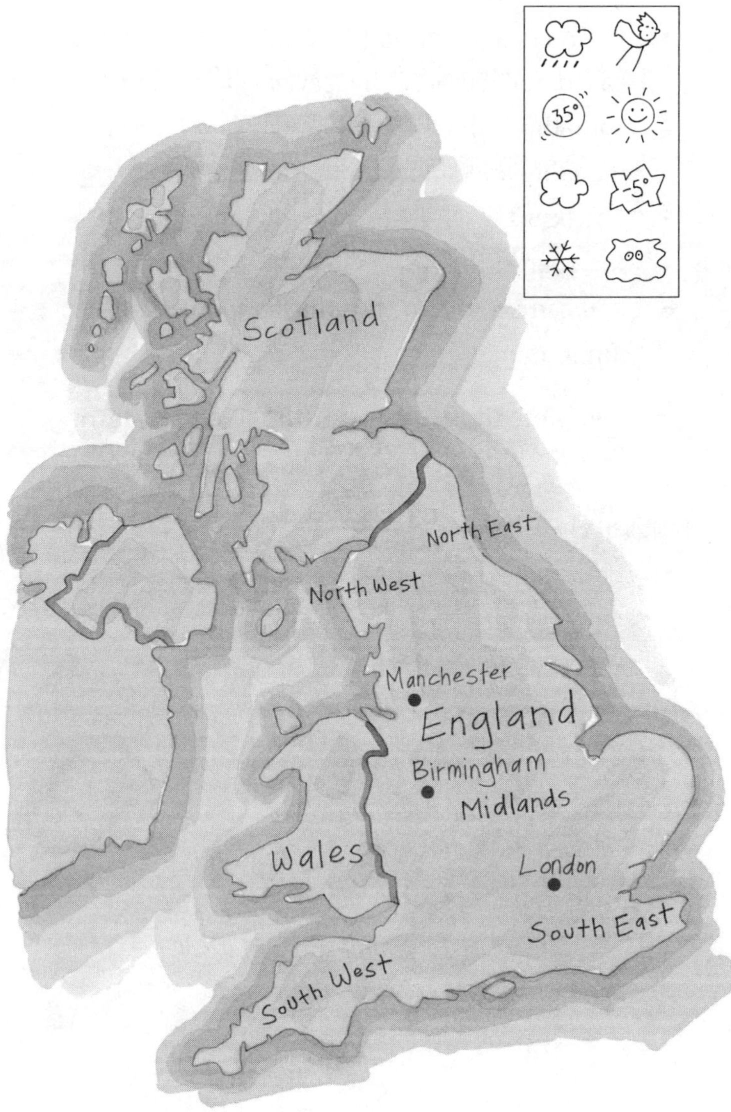

Your Turn

4 **Complete the sentences with true information.**

1 Today the weather is ______ in my town.
2 It's often ______ in the south of my country.
3 It's usually ______ on my birthday.
4 It's never ______ in January in my country.
5 I like the weather when it's ______ .
6 I hate the weather when it's ______ .

13 Vocabulary and Grammar

Vocabulary: Seasons

1 Put the letters in the correct order to complete the sentences.

1 When it's (eumrsm) *summer* in Europe, it's (riewtn) ________ in Australia.
2 In Europe, (pnsrig) ________ is the first season of the year.
3 In American English, (nuautm) ________ is called 'fall' because the leaves fall off the trees.
4 Sometimes there's a (abrniow) ________ when it's rainy and sunny at the same time.
5 The (ksy) ________ is really dark for a lot of the year in the Arctic Circle.
6 You can see the town from the top of the (uminotan) ________ .

2 Complete the sentences with the correct form of the words in brackets.

Word Builder

1 Oh no! There is a big black *cloud* in the sky. (cloudy)
2 There isn't any ________ in my country in the summer. (rainy)
3 Summer is my favourite season – I like ________ weather. (sun)
4 Look! There is ________ on all the trees. (snowy)
5 I can't cycle to school today – it's very ________ . (fog)
6 Be careful on your bike – it's very ________ today. (wind)

Grammar: Present Continuous (1)

➤ Grammar Reference, page 93–94

☆ **3 Write the *-ing* form of the verbs.**

1 enjoy – *enjoying*
2 stop – *stopping*
3 take – *taking*
4 do – ________
5 carry – ________
6 write – ________
7 run – ________
8 make – ________

19 ☆ **4 What are the activities? Listen and complete the sentences with the Present Continuous.**

1 The boys *are playing football.*
2 Dad ________ lunch.
3 The children ________ in the pool.
4 The girls ________ their bikes to town.
5 Liz ________ a shower.
6 Joe and Adam ________ to rap music.
7 I ________ to my favourite song.

☆☆ **5 Complete Ellen's email with the verbs in the Present Continuous.**

Hi Maddie,

How are things with you? I [1] *'m sitting* (sit) in my bedroom and I'm bored! I can't go out because I [2] ________ (not feel) very well. I [3] ________ (not enjoy) the weekend at all. It [4] ________ (not rain) but it's very cold. And I've got a lot of homework, but I [5] ________ (not do) it today.

Mum isn't here. She [6] ________ (not work) today because she [7] ________ (visit) my grandma. Dad [8] ________ (make) lunch. My brother is in his bedroom with his friends. They [9] ________ (play) computer games. And my sisters [10] ________ (have) fun with their friends too. It's horrible! Are you on your computer? Please email me soon!

Love,
Ellen

☆☆ **6** **Look at the picture. Correct the sentences with the verbs in the box. Use the Present Continuous.**

get in work stand run ~~rain~~ put on

1 The sun is shining. The sun *isn't shining* . It *'s raining.* .
2 The girls are running for the bus. They ______ . They ______ .
3 The man is carrying an umbrella. He ______ . He ______ .
4 The boy is walking across the park. He ______ . He ______ .
5 The woman is waiting at the bus stop. She ______ . She ______ .
6 The gardeners are going home. They ______ . They ______ .

Your Turn

☆☆☆ **7** **Think about your favourite photograph. Complete the description.**

I've got a photo of ______ (person). *It's* ______ (season) *and it's* ______ (weather). *In the photo, I* ______ (activity). ______ *and* ______ (people) ______ (activity). *I like the photo because it's* ______ (funny / interesting / cool).

8 **Write questions for the answers.**

Sentence Builder

1 *Why are you nervous?*
I'm nervous because I've got an exam.

2 ______
It's cold in here because the window is open.

3 ______
We don't want to go out because it's rainy.

4 ______
The dog is under the bed because he's scared of the rain.

5 ______
I want to go to the shopping centre because I need some new shoes.

6 ______
I need to use the computer because I'm doing my homework.

14 Vocabulary and Grammar

Grammar: Present Continuous (2)

➤ Grammar Reference, page 93–94

☆ **1 Write the questions correctly and add punctuation.**

1 whatareyoudoinginthekitchen
What are you doing in the kitchen?

2 whyaretheylookingatthesky

3 whoareyouwaitingfor

4 whereisyourfriendgoingnow

5 whatisdadmakingfordinner

6 whyisshewearingahatinthehouse

☆ **2 Write the words in the correct order.**

1 summer? / enjoying / you / Are / the
Are you enjoying the summer?

2 English? / studying / your / Is / sister

3 staying / York? / your / Are / friends / in

4 us / at / waiting / Is / home? / Dad / for

5 now? / using / Are / your / you / computer

6 in / mountains? / it / the / Is / snowing

☆☆ **3 Write the questions (1–6). Then match the answers (a–f).**

1 what / he / do / at the park
What is he doing at the park? [*b*]

2 where / you / go [ ]

3 they / play / tennis [ ]

4 you / enjoy / the film [ ]

5 he / do / his homework [ ]

6 why / you / run [ ]

a To the sports centre.
b He's meeting his friends.
c Yes, it's great.
d Yes, they are.
e Because I'm late for school.
f No, he isn't.

☆☆ **4 Complete the questions for the answers.**

1 What *are you studying?*

We're studying history.

2 What

My friends are hanging out at the beach.

3 What

She's wearing jeans and a T-shirt.

4 Where

I'm going to the city centre.

5 What

They're watching a Johnny Depp film.

6 Why

She's crying because she's watching a sad film.

☆☆ **5 Write the questions in the box in the correct place in the dialogue. There are two questions you don't need.**

a But why is everyone laughing?
b Are they eating something?
c What's she doing?
d Where are you standing in this photo?
~~**e** What are you doing?~~
f Are you having a good time?
g What's happening in this photo?

Tina [1] *e*
Ed I'm just looking at some photos. Come and have a look.
Tina OK. Oh, these are great. [2] ________
Ed We're at an adventure park. We're walking on a bridge up in the trees.
Tina Oh, that's exciting. And there's your sister. [3] ________
Ed She's coming down a zip slide – very fast! And here are some photos of Wales.
Tina [4] ________
Ed Er, we're on a mountain but it's very foggy, so you can't see very well.
Tina Oh, this is a good photo. [5] ________
Ed Because we've got ice creams and it's starting to rain.
Tina Oh, yes, I can just see the rain. Have a look at my homepage. I've got some new photos, too.

Your Turn

☆☆☆ **6 Write questions and true answers.**

1 it / rain
Is it raining?
Yes, it is. / No, it isn't.

2 what / you / wear
____
____

3 you and your friends / sit in your classroom
____
____

4 where / you / sit
____
____

5 your best friend / study with you
____
____

6 what / you / write with
____
____

7 the sun / shine
____
____

8 what / your parents / do
____
____

7 Change the words in *italics* to subject pronouns.

Sentence Builder

My family and I are at the beach. [1] ~~*My family and I*~~ *We* are enjoying the good weather. [2] *The weather* is hot and sunny. My sister is sitting near the water. [3] *My sister* is reading a magazine. Mum and Dad are sitting under an umbrella with my little brother. [4] *Mum and Dad* are playing with [5] *my brother*. Our dog has got a ball. He is running after [6] *the ball.*

15 Skills

Vocabulary: Food, drink and prices

1 Write the words under the correct headings.

Word Builder

~~cola~~ water sweets sun cream orange juice peanuts lemonade biscuits batteries crisps

 can of …	 a bottle of …	 a packet of …	 a carton of …
cola	*cola*	______	______
	______	______	
	______	______	
	______	______	
		______	

2 Write the prices in numbers or words.

1 seven pounds

£7.00

2 eighty-nine pence

3 one pound thirty-five

4 seven pounds ninety-nine

5 one pound ninety-nine

£1.99

6 ______

£5.75

7 ______

£49.63

8 ______

£119.99

Key Expressions: Shopping

3 Number the lines of the dialogue in the correct order.

Shop assistant	How many would you like?	☐
Customer	Thank you very much.	☐
Shop assistant	Yes, here you are. That's five pounds sixty, please.	☐
Customer	Yes, I'd like these biscuits, please.	☐
Shop assistant	Thank you. Bye.	*11*
Customer	Two, please. And how much are the big packets of crisps?	☐
Shop assistant	Certainly.	*3*
Customer	And have you got any cans of cola?	☐
Shop assistant	They're one pound fifty.	☐
Customer	Can I have two packets?	☐
Shop assistant	Hello. Can I help you?	*1*

Listening

20 **4** Listen to the dialogues and complete the table.

	Wants to buy	Spends
Customer 1	four stamps	£ *1.80*
Customer 2	postcards and a ______	£ ______
Customer 3	______ and crisps	£ ______
Customer 4	magazines and ______ cartons of ______	£ ______

Reading

5 Read the postcard and choose the correct answers.

Hi Mum and Dad,

I'm writing this in a small café in town. I'm looking out of the window at Rob and Emma. They're buying some magazines and taking photos. The weather isn't bad here – it isn't raining but there are some clouds in the sky. We can't go to the beach today but we're having a great time.

Phone me soon.

Claire x

View of Barcelona.

AFFIX STAMP HERE

Mr and Mrs Harper
189 Park Street
York
England

Printed in Spain.

1 Who is the postcard to?
 a Claire's friends **b** Claire **(c)** Claire's parents

2 Where are Mr and Mrs Harper?
 a in a hotel **b** at home **c** on holiday

3 What are Rob and Emma doing?
 a shopping **b** having a drink **c** going to the beach

4 What's the weather like?
 a sunny **b** wet **c** cloudy

5 Are the teenagers enjoying the visit?
 a No, they aren't. **b** Yes, but not very much. **c** Yes, very much.

Writing

6 Find and correct one mistake in each sentence.

1 I'm ~~writeing~~ writing this on a mountain in Croatia.

2 We don't taking photos of the mountains – it's very cloudy.

3 There are any interesting buildings in the town. It's very boring.

4 There isn't any snows, so we can't go skiing.

5 It's very foggy this morning, so we can't go walking.

6 I'm wears sun cream because it's very hot today.

7 Imagine you are visiting a foreign city with your school. Write a postcard to your family. Answer these questions.

- Where are you?
- What is the weather like?
- What are you and your friends doing?
- Are you enjoying the visit? Why / Why not?

Language Check 5

Vocabulary

1 Complete the names of the seasons and containers.

*s*pring
a can of cola

1 s________
2 a________
3 w________
4 a b________ of water
5 a p________ crisps
6 a c________ of orange juice

☐ / 6

2 Choose the correct words.

England has very different (weather) / season from Greece.

1 Be careful on the road. It's very *ice / icy*.
2 You don't need your jacket – it's *hot / wet* today.
3 Look! The *sun / sky* is just behind those clouds.
4 It's very *cloudy / clouds* in the mountains.
5 Don't go out this evening – it's very *fog / foggy*.
6 The *wind / windy* is very strong in the north today.
7 It's *cold / warm* in here. Please open the window.
8 There isn't any *rain / rainbow* in the summer months.
9 Is it *snow / snowy* in Scotland today?

☐ / 9

Grammar

3 Correct the underlined mistakes.

What do you doing? *are*

1 The students are writeing a story. ________
2 Where are they go now? ________
3 What are your brother doing? ________
4 Do you enjoying the party? ________
5 I'm no doing my homework now. ________
6 Am you using your computer? ________
7 Does he studying at the moment? ________

☐ / 7

4 Complete the telephone dialogue with the verbs in the Present Continuous.

Pete Hi, Amy. It's Pete. Is Dad at home?
Amy No, he isn't. He's *playing* (play) golf.
Pete And what [1]________ Mum [2]________ (do)?
Amy She's with her friend in town. They [3]________ (shop) for clothes. And I [4]________ (listen) to my new CD. What [5]________ you [6]________ (do)?
Pete I'm playing football with some friends but we [7]________ (not enjoy) it.
Amy Why?
Pete Because it [8]________ (rain) and I'm all wet!

☐ / 8

Key Expressions

5 Write the words in the correct order.

some / I / Can / please? / stamps / have
Can I have some stamps, please?

1 you? / I / Can / help
____
2 these / please. / like / sweets / I'd
____
3 you / stamps / the United States? / any / Have / got / for
____
4 like? / would / How / you / many
____
5 please. / five / That's / pounds / sixty-five,
____

☐ / 5

What's your score?

Module 5

☐ Vocabulary
☐ Grammar
☐ Key Expressions
☐ / 35

This is easy.
I need more practice.
This is difficult.

Module 6 Expeditions

Get Ready

Vocabulary: Transport

1 **Look at the pictures and complete the crossword.**

Down

Across

2 **Complete the lists with the words in Exercise 1.**

on land	in the air	on water
sledge		

Listening

21 **3** **Listen and match Amy, Jo and Daniel (1–3) to their favourite way to travel (a–d). There is one way to travel that you don't need.**

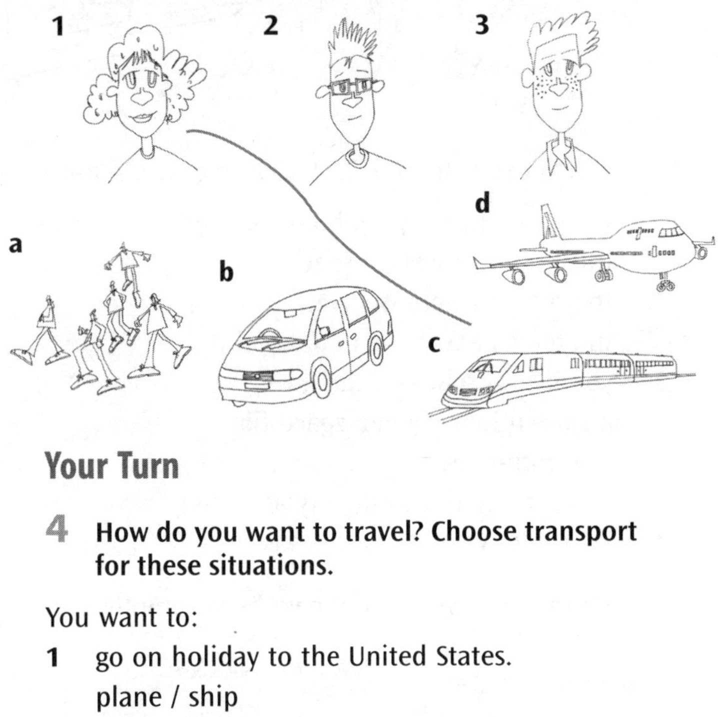

Your Turn

4 **How do you want to travel? Choose transport for these situations.**

You want to:

1 go on holiday to the United States.
plane / ship

2 show a visitor your town.
car / bus

3 travel across a river in your country.
canoe / ferry / balloon

4 travel across the Sahara Desert.
horse / camel / sledge

5 go to school in the snow.
car / bike / sledge

Vocabulary and Grammar

Vocabulary: Space

1 Label the picture with the words in the box.

astronaut crew Earth equipment oxygen ~~space station~~

2 Match the descriptions (1–8) to the words (a–h).

1 the group of people who work together on a spaceship — d
2 this person travels in space
3 the planet where we live
4 the tools people use to do a job
5 you live in space on this
6 a special journey in a spaceship
7 a scientific test
8 you can see this in the sky at night
9 we can't live without this gas

a experiment
b space station
c astronaut
d crew
e oxygen
f equipment
g Earth
h mission
i Moon

3 Make adjectives from the verbs to complete the sentences.

Word Builder

1 I'm *bored* with watching TV. (bore) ☐
2 I'm never ________ about exams. (worry) ☐
3 I'm always ________ after school. (tire) ☐
4 I'm ________ about my summer holidays. (excite) ☐
5 I'm not very ________ in fashion. (interest) ☐

4 Tick (✓) the sentences in Exercise 3 that are true for you.

Grammar: *was/were*

➤ Grammar Reference, page 94

☆ **5 Choose the correct words.**

1 There (*was*) / *were* a programme about space on TV last week.
2 The programme *was* / *were* about the International Space Station.
3 There *was* / *were* some interviews with scientists and astronauts.
4 The astronaut William Shepherd *was* / *were* in the programme.
5 The pictures of life on the space station *was* / *were* brilliant.
6 My friends *was* / *were* interested in the programme.

☆ **6 Write the verbs in the negative form.**

1 The first ISS mission ~~was~~ in the 1990s. *wasn't*
2 The astronauts were Chinese. ______
3 Buzz Aldrin was the commander. ______
4 There was a woman on the mission. ______
5 The astronauts were scared. ______
6 I was very interested in the mission. ______

☆☆ **7 How much do you know about space? Complete the questions with the question words and *was* or *were*. Then match the questions (1–7) to the answers (a–g).**

What	What	Who	~~Who~~	How many	Where	When

1 *Who* *was* the first woman in space? [*d*]
2 ______ ______ 'cosmonauts' from? [ ]
3 ______ ______ the first animal in space? [ ]
4 ______ nationality ______ the first man in space? [ ]
5 ______ ______ the first mission to the Moon? [ ]
6 ______ ______ astronauts ______ on the first mission to the Moon? [ ]
7 ______ ______ the first men on the Moon? [ ]

a Russia.
b Neil Armstrong and Buzz Aldrin.
c In 1969.
d Valentina Vladimirovna Tereshkova.
e Russian.
f Three.
g Laika, a dog.

Your Turn

☆☆ **8 Write true sentences.**

1 it hot / last week
It was hot last week. OR *It wasn't hot last week.*
2 I / at school yesterday
______
3 it cold / yesterday
______
4 my friends / at my house last night
______
5 I / worried about my last exams
______
6 my friends and I / in town last weekend
______

☆☆ **9 Write questions and true short answers.**

1 it / your birthday last month?
Was it your birthday last month?
Yes, it was. OR *No, it wasn't*
2 you / late for school yesterday?
______
______
3 you and your family / on holiday last July?
______
______
4 your mum / at work last weekend?
______
______
5 there / an English test last week?
______
______
6 you in bed / at 8 a.m. this morning?
______
______

17 Vocabulary and Grammar

Vocabulary: Verb + Noun

1 Complete the noun sets with the verbs in the box.

cross say ~~raise~~ go on carry

1 *raise* money / £40,000 / a million dollars
2 ________ the desert / the sea / the border
3 ________ a journey / a mission / holiday
4 ________ suitcases / equipment / a camera
5 ________ hello / goodbye / thank you

Grammar: Past simple (1)

➤ Grammar Reference, page 94–95

☆ **2 Write these sentences in the Past Simple.**

1 I want to go to Turkey.
I wanted to go to Turkey.
2 We enjoy our holiday in Argentina.
____
3 They love travelling by plane.
____
4 It rains a lot in the autumn.
____
5 The ferry crosses the sea three times a day.
____
6 You start the journey in New York.
____

☆ **3 Complete the sentences with the verbs in the box. Use the Past Simple.**

~~start~~ cross arrive carry like want travel

1 My family and I *started* our journey in North Africa.
2 We ________ with a guide.
3 We ________ our bags on our backs.
4 Our guide was very interesting and everyone really ________ him.
5 We ________ the desert by camel.
6 My sister ________ to sleep under the stars.
7 We ________ in the city tired but very happy.

☆☆ **4 Complete the text with the verbs in brackets. Use the Past Simple.**

Last summer our class [1] *decided* (decide) to go on an activity holiday. We [2] ________ (travel) by bus for five hours and [3] ________ (arrive) at the activity centre at night. We were all tired but very excited. The next day the activities [4] ________ (start) very early. In the morning, we [5] ________ (walk) for two hours along the river. We [6] ________ (watch) animals and birds, and then we [7] ________ (return) to the centre by bike. In the afternoon, I [8] ________ (want) to ride a horse. My best friend [9] ________ (cross) the river in a canoe. We [10] ________ (stay) at the centre for five days and I [11] ________ (love) every minute!

☆☆ **5 Complete the timeline with the verbs in the box. Use the Past Simple.**

~~travel~~	land	be	travel	arrive
want	climb	live	cross	describe

1260 Marco Polo [1] *travelled* to China.

1492 Christopher Columbus [2] __________ to go to Asia, but he arrived in Central America.

1768 James Cook explored the Pacific Ocean.

1846–48 Ida Pfeiffer [3] __________ round the world alone and [4] __________ her journeys in one of the first travel books.

1932 Amelia Earhart [5] __________ the Atlantic Ocean by plane.

1953 Sir Edmund Hillary [6] __________ Mount Everest.

1969 Neil Armstrong [7] __________ on the Moon in the Apollo 11 mission.

1986 Ann Bancroft [8] __________ the first woman to travel to the North Pole on foot.

2001 Susan J. Helms [9] __________ on the ISS for 147 days. She was the first female astronaut to do this.

2009 Mike Perham [10] __________ home after sailing round the world. He was only 17 years old.

☆☆ **6 Read the information in the advert. Then complete Kati's email of her holiday.**

Visit Croatia for a fantastic holiday.

- Stay in the capital Zagreb or rent a traditional house on the coast.
- Sunbathe on the beach or try diving in the clear Adriatic Sea.
- Explore the Old Town in Dubrovnik, a UNESCO World Heritage Site.
- Walk around the Plitvice Lakes National Park and enjoy the beautiful scenery.

Hi Viktor,

Thanks for your email. You asked about my holiday. Well, I [1] *visited* Croatia for the first time with my family last month. It [2] __________ fantastic. We [3] __________ a traditional house on the coast. The weather was great so we [4] __________ on the beach. I also [5] __________ diving for the first time! We [6] __________ the Old Town in Dubrovnik. It was really interesting. We also [7] __________ around the Plitvice Lakes National Park and I really [8] __________ the scenery.

Kati

Your Turn

☆☆☆ **7 Complete the description with true information about one of your holidays.**

In __________ (*year*) *I* __________ (travel) *to* __________ (*country/city*) *with* __________ (*people*). *We* __________ (stay) *in a* __________ (*place*). *We* __________ (visit) __________ (*place*). *It* __________ (be) __________ (*adjective*). *We also* __________ (explore) __________ (*place*). *The people there* __________ (be) __________ (*adjective*).

18 Skills

Key Expressions: Suggestions

1 Match the suggestions (1–5) to the replies (a–e).

1 It's getting dark. Why don't we take some photos now?
2 We can get some water from the river.
3 Let's finish that packet of biscuits.
4 Why don't you phone home?
5 Let's stop for a minute.

a No, I can't. The battery on my mobile is low.
b Right, let's do that. Here's the camera.
c That's a good idea. This climbing is hard work.
d No, not now. We can't eat everything.
e That's not a very good idea. It looks really dirty.

2 Match the words in A and B to make phrases. Then use them to write suggestions for the situations.

A check	change	~~put up~~	phone	put on

B for help	the batteries	some sun cream	~~the tents~~	the map

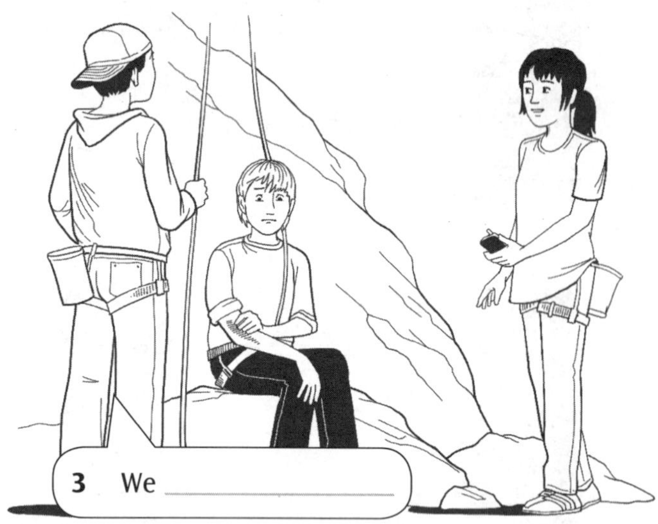

Listening

22 **3 Listen to Sally and Leo planning an expedition. Which objects can each person take?**

People			Objects	
1	Sally	*c*	a	map
2	Leo		b	sun cream
3	Anne		c	tent
4	Jim		d	torch
5	Sue		e	cooking equipment
			g	camera
			f	compass

Reading

4 Read Tom's email and his friends' replies. Write the correct names.

1 ___*Tom*___ goes to Scotland every year.
2 __________ doesn't want to go to Scotland.
3 __________ enjoyed a holiday in Spain.
4 __________ tried different activities on holiday.
5 __________ wants to go on holiday with Tom.

From: [Tom_Hardy@tomemail.co.uk]

Hi Lucy and Mike,
My parents want to go on holiday to Scotland but we always go there. It's so boring! What can I do?
Tom

Hi Tom,
Don't worry about your holiday. There are lots of interesting places to visit. We visited Spain last summer. It was fantastic. Why don't you ask your parents to go there?
Good luck!
Lucy

Hi Tom,
I've got an idea. We were on an activity holiday in France last year. There was swimming, horse riding and canoeing. I want to go again this year so maybe you can come with me. Why don't we ask your parents?
Mike

Writing

5 Write the words in the correct order. Add the correct punctuation.

Sentence Builder

1 last weekend / my sister's / it was / birthday
It was my sister's birthday last weekend.
2 yesterday / my grandparents / i visited
____
3 last night / watched a good film / we
____
4 i / last year / enjoyed my holiday in italy
____
5 studied for an english test / we / last week
____
6 this morning / i / stayed in bed late
____

6 Complete the sentences with true information.

1 My school ___*was closed*___ last month.
2 I __________ yesterday.
3 My friend __________ last night.
4 My family __________ last weekend.
5 I __________ this morning.
6 My lessons __________ last week.

7 Write a short email to Tom.

- Say where you visited on holiday last year and when.
- Suggest a good place for Tom's holiday.

Reading Corner 3

Expeditions

1 Look at the title, the map and the photos. What do you think the text is about?

a a family holiday in Africa
b an expedition to help an animal in danger
c collecting animals for zoos

Serious Desert

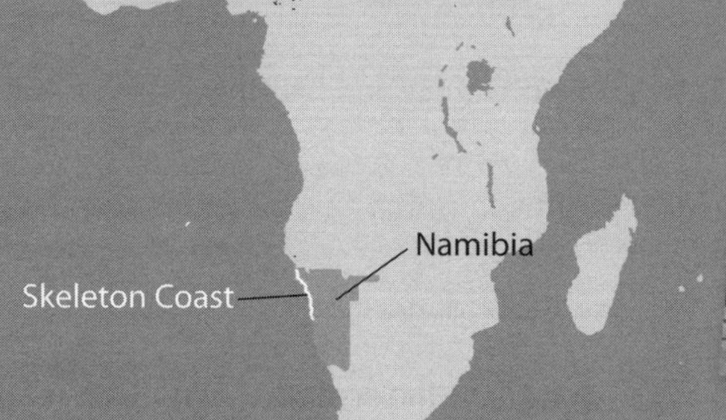

In 2003 eight teenagers were on an expedition called 'Serious Desert'. They travelled to Namibia in South-West Africa to help the black rhino, an animal that is very rare.

More than 6,500 teenagers wanted to go on 'Serious Desert' but there were only eight winners. They passed some difficult tests in England. They started by swimming in a cold lake, climbed high ropes and camped in strong winds. They also touched snakes and scorpions but they weren't scared!

The group were in Namibia from 13th April to 5th May, and there were lots of challenges. They travelled long distances, constructed camps, and tried strange food. They tracked black rhinos and collected useful information about them. The weather was also a problem. It was very hot in the day – sometimes 40°C. At night, there were no clouds in the sky so it was very cold. At the start of the expedition, there was even a lot of rain!

In the last week, the teenagers crossed the desert on foot to the Skeleton Coast. Their camels carried all their clothes and equipment. This was a difficult journey because the dunes were very high. When the group arrived at the coast, they raced into the Atlantic Ocean for a swim. A fantastic end to a fantastic expedition!

2 **Read the text quickly and check your answer to Exercise 1.**

3 **Read the text again and answer true (T) or false (F).**

1 A lot of people wanted to go on the expedition. T
2 The winners passed a geography test about Africa. ☐
3 The group was in Africa for three weeks. ☐
4 They stayed in hotels on the expedition. ☐
5 The weather changed very often. ☐
6 The group went to sleep when they arrived at the coast. ☐

4 **Match to the numbers from the text (1–6) to the descriptions (a–f).**

1	2003	**a**	the start of the expedition
2	over 6,500	**b**	the number of teenagers who wanted to go
3	eight	**c**	the temperature during the day
4	13 April	**d**	the end of the expedition
5	5 May	**e**	the year of 'Serious Desert'
6	40°	**f**	the number of winners

5 **Find these words in the text.**

1 five words to talk about the weather
winds ______ ______ ______ ______

2 four animals
______ ______ ______ ______

6 **Find the words in the text for these definitions.**

1 unusual (paragraph 1)
______

2 you use these to help you get up a mountain (paragraph 2)
______

3 followed (paragraph 3)
______

4 tools and useful objects (paragraph 4)
______

5 hills of sand (paragraph 4)
______

7 **Read Martin's blog and choose the correct answers.**

Extreme Desert Blog
http://www.extreme-desert-blog.com

21 April
Hi, it's Martin here again. Guess what? We were really close to a black rhino today. Aimee and I were on a rhino trek with Bruce, the expedition leader. We noticed some new footprints. It was so exciting because there weren't any rhinos in the first week. It was fantastic when the rhino appeared and walked past us. It was amazing because it's very rare. You can't often see black rhinos in zoos. To see the rhino in Namibia was an experience I will never forget.

posted at 11:45 (2) comments

1 Martin updated his blog
a on the expedition. (circled)
b after the expedition.

2 How many people were with Martin on the rhino trek?
a two
b three

3 Who do you think Aimee is?
a another teenager
b the leader of the expedition

4 The first thing they noticed
a was a rhino.
b were the tracks of a rhino.

5 Why was Martin excited about the rhino?
a There was one in a zoo.
b There aren't many rhinos.

6 What does Martin say about his experience?
a He will always remember it.
b He wants to forget it.

8 **Answer the questions.**

1 What do you think of the eight teenagers? Use these adjectives or your own ideas:

interesting	cool	great	boring
nervous	dangerous	lucky	brave

I think they're ______ .

2 Would you like to go on an expedition to Africa?
______

3 What animals are in danger in your country?
______

Language Check 6

Vocabulary

1 Read the descriptions and complete the words.

You travel on water in this. s *h i p*

1 You ride on this in the desert. c _ _ _ _
2 You travel on water in this. f _ _ _ _
3 You travel in the air in this. b _ _ _ _ _ _
4 You travel from city to city in this. t _ _ _ _
5 You can travel in the snow on this. s _ _ _ _ _
6 You can live in space on this. s _ _ _ _ s _ _ _ _ _ _
7 This person travels in space. a _ _ _ _ _ _ _ _
8 This is the group of people on a spaceship. c _ _ _
9 This is a scientific test. e _ _ _ _ _ _ _ _ _
10 This is our planet. E _ _ _ _
11 You do this for charity. r _ _ _ _ m _ _ _ _
12 You do this when you leave. s _ _ g _ _ _ _ _ _
13 You feel this after a long walk. t _ _ _ _
14 You feel this before your birthday. e _ _ _ _ _ _
15 You sometimes feel this before an exam. w _ _ _ _ _ _

☐ / 15

Grammar

2 Complete the dialogue with *was*, *wasn't*, *were* or *weren't*.

A Where *were* you yesterday? You ¹______ at the football match.
B I ²______ in bed because I ³______ very well. ⁴______ the match good?
A Yes, it ⁵______ great.
B What ⁶______ the score?
A 4–2 to us. We ⁷______ brilliant in the first half and the teachers ⁸______ really happy with the score.

☐ / 8

3 Complete Kim's email with the verbs in brackets. Use the Past Simple.

Hi David,
You *asked* (ask) me about my expedition to Scotland. Well, we ¹______ (travel) to the north of Scotland by bus but after that we ²______ (walk), ³______ (climb) mountains and ⁴______ (cross) the river by canoe!

All the activities were great but it was hard work, too. I ⁵______ (carry) water from the river every evening and ⁶______ (cook) on a fire at the camp. Our leader ⁷______ (play) the guitar under the stars!

There's some information about the expedition on our school website. Why don't you look at it? There's a photo of me in the river!

See you soon.
Kim

☐ / 7

Key Expressions

4 Choose the correct words.

A I'm *tired* / *(bored)*. ¹*Let's* / *Can* go for a walk.
B No, we ²*can't* / *can*. It's really cold.
A Okay, why ³*do* / *don't* we go to the cinema?
B No, not ⁴*no* / *now*. It's closed.
A Well, we can go shopping.
B ⁵*That's* / *That* not a very good idea. I haven't got any money.

☐ / 5

What's your score?

Module 6

☐ Vocabulary
☐ Grammar
☐ Key Expressions
☐ / 35

This is easy.
I need more practice.
This is difficult.

Module 7 Helping

Get Ready

Vocabulary: Helping

1 Complete the poster with the words in the box.

~~the community~~ water save tins animals turn off bottles environment taps recycle

Listening

23 2 Listen and match the actions (a–f) to the people (1–6).

1	Emma	a	save water
2	Joe	b	help animals
3	Sally	c	turn off lights
4	Eddie	d	recycle batteries
5	Kelly	e	save electricity
6	Greg	f	help the community

(Example: 1 Emma – e)

Your Turn

3 Match the words in A and B to write true sentences.

A ~~tidy~~ empty clean do save recycle

B the bins the car ~~my room~~ paper the washing-up electricity

1 *I tidy my room every week.*
2 ________
3 ________
4 ________
5 ________
6 ________

19 Vocabulary and Grammar

Vocabulary: Animals

1 **Match the names of the animals (1–9) to the pictures (a–i).**

c
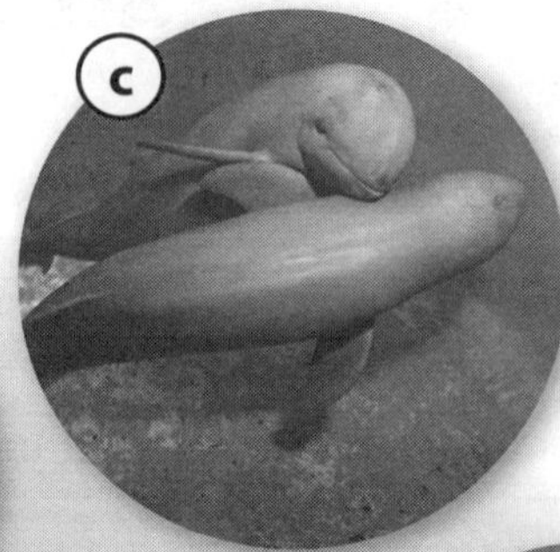

a

b

d

e

1 bald eagle
2 panda
3 gorilla
4 Amur tiger
5 blue whale
6 sloth
7 black rhino
8 Irrawaddy dolphin
9 polar bear

f

g

h

i

2 **Write sentences using *with*.**

Sentence Builder

1 It's a small house. It's got a garden.
It's a small house with a garden.

2 It's a small mobile phone. It's got a camera.
____

3 It's a comfortable hotel. It's got a swimming pool.
____

4 It's a new shopping centre. It's got a café.
____

5 She's a tall girl. She's got dark hair.
____

6 He's a young footballer. He's got great skills.
____

Grammar: Past Simple (2)

➤ Grammar Reference, page 94–95

☆ **3** **Write the verbs under the correct headings. Then write the Past Simple of the irregular verbs.**

~~live~~ ~~find~~ ask take work give increase have buy save kill go see help

Regular	Irregular	Past Simple
live	*find*	*found*

☆ **4 Tick (✓) the correct sentences and correct the mistakes in the incorrect sentences.**

1 We ~~do~~ an interesting project on animals last month. *did*
2 Our teacher gave us some surprising information. ✓
3 A wildlife expert cames to our school. ______
4 My friend wroted some notes on whales and dolphins. ______
5 I learnt a lot about changes in animal habitat. ______
6 The art class drew some pictures. ______
7 We putted up some wildlife posters on the classroom walls. ______

☆☆ **5 Complete the sentences with the verbs in the box. Use the Past Simple.**

~~become~~ find begin think meet say fall

1 The Quagga, half horse and half zebra, *became* extinct in 1883.
2 Scientists ______ that the Siamese Crocodile was extinct, but someone ______ a picture of one in a magazine in 2001.
3 The World Wildlife Fund ______ its work with animals in 1961.
4 Leaders of 13 countries ______ in 2010, the Year of the Tiger, to discuss the future of this endangered animal.
5 A report in 2010 ______ that large animals in Africa's national parks were in danger. The population of important species ______ by nearly 60% between 1970 and 2005.

☆☆ **6 Complete the description with the phrases in the box. Use the Past Simple.**

~~write a book~~ do some research read a lot of books become interested come to Alaska begin to work spend two months catch young bears go to the zoo

Jeni Braddock was born in Florida but now she lives in Alaska. Last year she [1] *wrote a book* about her work with polar bears.

"I [2] ______ in animals when I was a child. I [3] ______ to see the animals every week and I [4] ______ about wildlife. Florida was always warm and sunny but I wanted to live in a snowy place! I [5] ______ in 1995 and I studied biology at the university here. I [6] ______ in the Arctic in 2005."

Last year Jeni [7] ______ into the polar bears in the Arctic Circle.

"My team and I [8] ______ out on the ice. We [9] ______, weighed them and checked their health. The area is changing a lot and it's getting difficult for the bears. I wanted people to understand the Arctic so I decided to write my book."

Your Turn

☆☆☆ **7 Write true sentences about last Friday.**

1 I / sleep (number of hours)
I slept for eight hours.
2 I / get up (*time*)
______
3 my friends and I / get to school (*time*)
______
4 I / have (*food*) for lunch
______
5 my mum / give me (*object*)
______
6 I / meet my friends (*place*) after school
______

20 Vocabulary and Grammar

Vocabulary: Problems

1 Complete the poem with the words in the box.

bullying ~~traffic~~ graffiti litter vandalism

^{1} *Traffic* in the city
It really isn't pretty
^{2} ________ on the walls
And shop front doors
^{3} ________ in the streets
Under our feet
Broken glass in the park
Don't go there after dark
^{4} ________ at school
It just isn't cool
^{5} ________ everywhere
Lots of things to repair
We want a nice place to live,
Safe and attractive.
We can make our city great,
It's never too late!

2 Choose a title for the poem in Exercise 1.

a Helping the community
b Don't forget to recycle
c Our city needs you

Grammar: Past Simple (3)

➤ Grammar Reference, page 94–95

☆ **3 Complete the sentence beginnings with the verbs in the box. Use the Past Simple negative. Then match the reasons (a–f) to the sentence beginnings (1–6) to make full sentences.**

~~collect~~ ride start want meet drive

1 We didn't *collect* much litter [*c*]
2 I ________ to pick up litter [ ]
3 She ________ her friends after school [ ]
4 Dad ________ the car into town [ ]
5 Adam ________ his bike in the park [ ]
6 We ________ work at 10 a.m. [ ]

because
a there was too much traffic.
b some people were late.
~~**c** there weren't many volunteers.~~
d the weather was wet.
e there was a lot of broken glass.
f there weren't any safe places to go.

☆☆ **4 Look at the information about a volunteering day. Correct the information in the sentences.**

Hilltop School Volunteering Day
Time: 10 a.m. Place: City Park

Jobs	Names
clean graffiti off walls	*Ana, Liam*
collect litter	*Eddie, Kim*
plant flowers	*Diane*
build bird boxes	*Rani*
collect money for charity	*Matt*

1 The students met at 10.30.
They *didn't meet at 10.30. They met at 10 o'clock.*
2 They worked in town.
They ________
3 Ana and Liam collected litter.
They ________
4 Diane collected money for charity.
She ________
5 Matt planted flowers.
He ________
6 Eddie and Kim built bird boxes.
They ________
7 Rani cleaned graffiti off walls.
She ________

☆☆ **5** **Complete the interview with the correct form of the words in brackets. Use Past Simple questions and short answers.**

Reporter So, tell me about your volunteering day. Where [1] *did* you *work* (work)?

Ana We were in the City Park for a day.

Reporter Okay, and what job [2] ______ you ______ (do), Ana?

Ana I cleaned graffiti off the walls of the café.

Reporter Very good. And [3] ______ you ______ (do) that too, Liam?

Liam Yes, I [4] ______ . It was hard work but the café looks really good now.

Reporter Great. And what about the rest of you? How [5] ______ you ______ (help)?

Kim Eddie and I collected a lot of litter.

Diane And I planted some flowers.

Reporter And you, Rani? [6] ______ you ______ (work) with Diane?

Rani No, I [7] ______ . I built some bird boxes and put them in the trees.

Reporter Oh, why [8] ______ you ______ (do) that?

Rani I just wanted to help the local wildlife. But Matt was brilliant. He collected a lot of money for charity.

Reporter Really? How much [9] ______ you ______ (collect), Matt?

Matt About eighty pounds.

Reporter That's brilliant. Well done, all of you. Now, last question. [10] ______ your teachers ______ (help) you?

All No, they [11] ______ !

Miss Trent That's not true! We worked very hard.

Ana Oh, hello, Miss Trent … sorry.

Your Turn

☆☆ **6** **Write questions and true answers.**

1 you / see your friends / last night?
Did you see your friends last night?
Yes, I did. OR *No, I didn't.*

2 where / you / go / last weekend?
Where did you go last weekend?
I went to the skatepark.

3 your team / win / their last match?
______
______

4 where / your family / go / last summer?
______
______

5 your best friend / text you / last night?
______
______

6 what subjects / your class / study yesterday?
______
______

7 your teacher / give you a lot of homework / last week?
______
______

☆☆☆ **7** **Imagine you had the perfect birthday. Write what you did and didn't do. Use the verbs in the box or your own ideas.**

get up go to school eat make my bed watch buy tidy my room play do my homework go shopping go out have a party go to bed

My last birthday was fantastic. In the morning, I ______ at ______ . I ______ . I didn't ______ or ______ . In the afternoon, my friends and I ______ and ______ . We didn't ______ . In the evening, my family and I ______ . We didn't ______ . I ______ at ______ .

21 Skills

Vocabulary: Animals

1 Picture Dictionary **page 110 of the Student's Book. Read the descriptions and write the names of the animals.**

CITY ANIMAL CENTRE Open Day

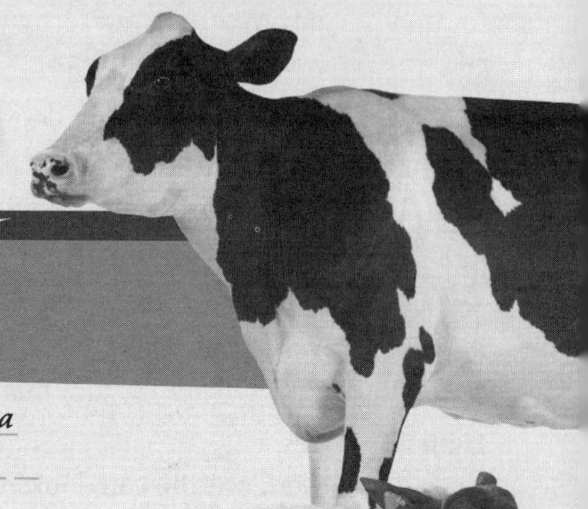

What do you know about animals at the centre?
Try our quiz and find out!

1 This is a large type of lizard. *iguana*
2 This animal is very slow. __________
3 You get milk from this animal. ___
4 This animal has small horns and a beard. ____
5 You can ride this animal. _____
6 This animal can be very fat. ___
7 You get wool from this animal. _____
8 This bird lives on water. ____
9 This animal has red-brown fur and a thick tail. ___
10 You can take this animal for a walk. ___
11 The tiger is a wild example of this animal. ___
12 This animal has long ears and soft fur. ______
13 You get eggs from this bird. ___

The City Animal Centre needs volunteers.
Have fun and help the animals.
Come to the Information Desk to find out more.

Key Expressions: Requests

2 **Match a line from each column, (1–6) to (a–f) to (i–vi) to make dialogues.**

1 I need to phone my mum.
2 I'm hungry.
3 I don't understand this word.
4 I'm tired.
5 I can't do my homework.
6 Collecting litter is boring.

a Can you pass me the dictionary, please?
b Can I sit down, please?
c Can you help me with this exercise, please?
d Can I do a different job, please?
e Can I have a sandwich, please?
f Can I use your mobile, please?

i Okay, just a second. Brown or white bread?
ii No, I'm sorry, you can't. We need to clean up this area.
iii Sure, no problem. Have my chair.
iv No, I'm sorry, you can't. My battery's low.
v Sure, no problem. Which question don't you understand?
vi Sure, here you are.

Listening

24 **3 Listen and choose the correct information.**

1 Jane helps her mum with *the cooking / the dishes*.
2 Jim is eating *biscuits / crisps*.
3 Kelly *can / can't* use Dave's skateboard.
4 Rachel is helping at *home / school*.
5 Liz *wants / doesn't want* to help her neighbour.
6 Vicky *can / can't* use Paul's Spanish book.

Reading

4 Read the email and answer true (T) or false (F).

Hi Josh,
Thanks for your message. You asked about our Charity Day. Well, it was last Sunday in the town centre. The day started with some races between teachers and students. And the students won! After that, there was face-painting and then a magic show for the children. At lunchtime, we sold sandwiches and home-made cakes.

After lunch, there was a concert with different singers and musicians. I played in the school jazz band. Then we had a fashion show with models from the local schools. After that, there was a quiz with a prize of a weekend in London.

After dark, there were fireworks and a barbecue. We had a great day and we raised £1250 for disabled children. I hope this gives you some ideas for your Charity Day!

Good luck!
Natalie

1 Natalie wanted information about Josh's Charity Day. ☐
2 The first activity of the day was sport. ☐
3 There weren't any activities for young children. ☐
4 Natalie wasn't part of the concert. ☐
5 The Charity Day continued into the evening. ☐
6 They raised more than a thousand pounds for charity. ☐

5 Choose the correct words.

Sentence Builder

We arrived at the Charity Day. First there was a fancy dress competition and [1]*after / then* we watched skateboarders. [2]*Then / After* that, there was a dance show. [3]*After / Then* lunch we bought some home-made biscuits and sweets. [4]*Then / After* we did a quiz and my friend won a prize.

Your Turn

6 Complete the sentences with true information about last Monday. Use *then* or *after* in each sentence.

1 I arrived at school and ______ .
2 I had lessons and ______ .
3 ______ lunch, I ______ .
4 I went home and ______ .
5 ______ dinner, my family and I ______ .
6 ______ my homework, I ______ .
7 I brushed my teeth and ______ .

Writing

7 Read the first part of the email. Find and correct seven mistakes.

Hi Millie,
Thanks for you message. You asked for our Charity Day. Well, it was last Saterday at our school. The day begin with a football match between parents and teachers. After there were a painting competition and my friend winned a prize! We haved a gymnastic display and then lunch. …

8 Continue the email in Exercise 7. Answer these questions.

- What did you do in the afternoon?
- What did you do in the evening?
- How much did you raise for charity?

Language Check 7

Vocabulary

1 Write the words in the correct group.

~~paper~~ electricity the environment lights plastic tins water taps the community bottles

Recycle: *paper* ______
Save: ______
Turn off: ______
Help: ______

☐ / 9

2 Write the names of the animals.

1  ______

2  ______

3  ______

4  ______

5  ______

6  ______

7  ______

☐ / 7

Grammar

3 Complete the sentences with the verbs in the box. Use the Past Simple negative.

~~buy~~ eat watch go send see come

We went to the music shop, but I didn't buy *a CD.*

1 I had a party but my best friend ______ .
2 I was very tired but I ______ to bed.
3 We went to New York but we ______ the Statue of Liberty.
4 Mike wrote a letter but he ______ it.
5 Annie bought a DVD but she ______ it.
6 I made you a cake but you ______ it.

☐ / 6

4 Complete the dialogue with the verbs in brackets. Use the Past Simple.

A What *did* you *do* (do) last weekend?
B We went to a Charity Day.
A [1] ______ you ______ (have) a good time?
B Yes, we [2] ______ .
A How much [3] ______ they ______ (raise) for charity?
B About £500, I think. What about you? [4] ______ you ______ (go) away for the weekend?
A No, I [5] ______ but I went out on Saturday evening.
B Where [6] ______ you ______ (go)?
A I went to the new cinema.
B What [7] ______ you ______ (see)?
A The new Johnny Depp film.
B What [8] ______ you ______(think) of it?
A It was great. I really enjoyed it.

☐ / 8

Key Expressions

5 Complete the dialogues with the words in the box.

can't sorry help ~~use~~ here second

A Can I *use* your pen, please?
B Sure. [1] ______ you are.
A Can you [2] ______ me with my bags?
B OK, just a [3] ______ .
A Can I use your computer, please?
B No, I'm [4] ______ you [5] ______ . I'm using it.

☐ / 5

What's your score?

Module 7

☐ Vocabulary
☐ Grammar
☐ Key Expressions

☐ / 35

This is easy.
I need more practice.
This is difficult.

Module 8 Television

Get Ready

Vocabulary: TV programmes

1 **Match the TV programmes in the box to the opinions.**

cartoons	chat shows	documentaries	drama series
films	game shows	music programmes	news
reality shows	sitcoms	~~soaps~~	sports programmes

1 I hate them. The stories are boring and the actors aren't very good.
soaps

2 They are on TV a lot but I don't watch them. I prefer to see famous people on TV.
____

3 I watch all of them but my favourite is *The Simpsons*. I love the characters.
____

4 I think they can be a bit boring but I watch them when they are about animals.
____

5 I watch it once a day. It's important to know about changes in the world.
____

6 I watch them when my favourite football and basketball teams are on.
____

7 I enjoyed all *The Matrix* stories. The stunts and action scenes were fantastic.
____

8 I watch them with my family. We answer all the questions and have a competition.
____

9 My favourites were American – *Frasier* and *Friends*. They were so funny.
____

10 I love the interviews with actors. My favourite was Kirsten Dunst. She was really interesting.
____

11 I watch them every morning. It's great to see new groups and listen to my favourite songs.
____

12 My favourites are about detectives. I watch them every week and I never miss a programme.
____

Listening

25 **2** **Listen to the survey about TV programmes and complete the information. Are you the same as Fiona or Mike?**

TV survey

Name	Fiona	Mike
Number of hours of TV a day	*1.5*	_____
TV in bedroom?	yes / no	yes / no
Favourite kinds of programmes	_____, _____	_____, _____
Never watch	_____, _____	_____, _____

Your Turn

3 **Imagine that you have your own TV channel. Plan the programmes and times for this evening.**

6.00 *music programme*
6.00 __________
6.30 __________
_____ __________
_____ __________
_____ __________
_____ __________

22 Vocabulary and Grammar

Vocabulary: Adjectives

1 Choose the correct words.

Word Builder

1. Are you *interested* / *interesting* in music programmes?
2. We saw an *amazed* / *amazing* documentary on space.
3. I'm *bored* / *boring*. Turn on the TV, please.
4. Was the last James Bond film *excited* / *exciting*?
5. I never watch chat shows – I think they're *bored* / *boring*.
6. The reality show wasn't very *interesting* / *interested*.

Your Turn

2 Complete the sentences with true information.

1. I'm bored when I watch ______________ .
2. I think ______________ is an amazing film.
3. I like TV but I think ______________ shows are boring.
4. I was excited when I watched ______________ .

Grammar: Comparatives and superlatives

➤ Grammar Reference, page 95–96

☆ **3 Correct the underlined mistakes.**

1. Modern films are more exciting <u>that</u> old films. *than*
2. The second series was <u>more long</u> than the first. ______________
3. TV screens are much <u>biger</u> today. ______________
4. Is your new TV <u>easyer</u> to use? ______________
5. American soaps are <u>more funnyer</u> than soaps in my country. ______________
6. I think reality shows are the <u>more</u> interesting programmes. ______________
7. Why was the film <u>most interested</u> than the book? ______________
8. Prizes on game shows are much <u>gooder</u> today. ______________

26 ☆☆ **4 Listen and complete the table about two TVs.**

	AV1	HDZ
Screen (cm)	1 *82* cm	2 ______ cm
Colour	3 ______	good
Sound	not 4 ______	excellent
Easy to use?	yes	5 ______
Price	6 £ ______	7 £ ______

☆☆ **5 Correct the information about the TVs in Exercise 4 using comparatives.**

1. The HDZ is small.
   No, *it's bigger than the AV1.*
2. The colour on the HDZ is brilliant.
   No, ______________________ .
3. The sound on the HDZ isn't bad.
   No, ______________________ .
4. The AV1 is complicated.
   No, ______________________ .
5. The HDZ is cheap.
   No, ______________________ .

☆☆ **6 Write sentences using superlatives and your opinions.**

1. boring / programme on TV
   The most boring programme on TV is the news.
2. good / actor
   ____
3. popular / TV presenter
   ____
4. the singer / with the nice voice
   ____
5. bad / day for TV
   ____
6. interesting / chat show
   ____
7. big / cinema in my town
   ____
8. funny / programme on TV
   ____

☆☆ **7 Complete the quiz with superlatives. Then match the answers (a–g) to the questions (1–7).**

1 Where's *the largest* (large) film studio? [c]
2 What was one of __________ (popular) films in 2010? [ ]
3 Who won __________ (good) actress award at the 2010 Oscars? [ ]
4 How long was __________ (long) TV quiz programme? [ ]
5 When did __________ (early) public TV service start? [ ]
6 Who was __________ (young) TV presenter? [ ]

a 30th September, 1929, by the BBC, London
b Sandra Bullock for *The Blind Side*
c Ramoji Film City, India
d Australian Luis Tanner, aged 6
e Avatar, directed by James Cameron
f 52 hours, 45 minutes on channel 9Live, Germany

☆☆ **8 Complete the review with the correct form of the adjectives in brackets.**

TV blog

Adam's TV blog

219 followers Archive

Saturday was [1] *the best* (good) night for TV last week. The presenter of *Talk Talk* was [2] __________ (young) than on other chat shows but the guests were much [3] __________ (good). Usain Bolt won the athletics again. He was so much [4] __________ (fast) than the others. He's one of [5] __________ (successful) athletes in the world.
But the [6] __________ (funny) programme of the evening was a new sitcom called *Best of Friends*. It had some of [7] __________ (talented) young actors on TV at the moment.

Your Turn

☆☆ **9 Complete the opinions in the Internet chat room with comparatives or superlatives. Write your replies.**

chatroom

post reply

1 The *easiest* (easy) language to learn is English.
Yes, you're right. OR
Don't be silly. The easiest language to learn is Spanish.

2 Rap is __________ (good) than heavy metal.
____

3 The __________ (difficult) school subject is physics.
____

4 American films are __________ (funny) than films from other countries.
____

5 Reading is __________ (interesting) than watching TV.
____

6 The __________ (bad) singer in the world is Madonna.
____

7 Life in the country is __________ (safe) than life in the city.
____

Contact Us Top of Page
post reply

☆☆☆ **10 Complete the text with true information. Use the adjectives and verbs in the correct form.**

I *didn't see* (not see) a film at the cinema last Saturday. I __________ (watch) about __________ (*number of hours*) of TV. I __________ (watch) __________ (*kind of programme*) and __________ (*kind of programme*). I __________ (not watch) __________ (*type of programme*). The __________ (good) programme of the day was __________. I __________ (think) it was __________ (*adjective*). The __________ (bad) programme of the day was __________. I __________ (think) it was __________ (*adjective*).

23 Vocabulary and Grammar

Vocabulary: Future plans

1 Complete the noun sets with the verbs in the box.

be ~~go~~ worry about make help

1 *go* ______
around the world • to university • on holiday

2 ______
the future • my exams • the planet

3 ______
animals • the community • the environment

4 ______
a film • money • a difference to the world

5 ______
on TV • a fashion designer • famous

Grammar: *going to*

➤ Grammar Reference, page 96

27 ☆☆ **2 Listen to the chat show interview with four young actors. Complete the information.**

	Going to …
Josh	go to [1] *Jamaica* in [2] ______ go to the [3] ______ every day and relax be at [4] ______ in London
Maya	spend time with her [5] ______ stay with her mum and dad for a [6] ______ take [7] ______ test in September
Rob & Adele	work in a [8] ______ in Peru help to [9] ______ a school help teachers and students with their [10] ______

☆☆ **3 Correct the information in the sentences.**

1 Josh is going to go to Jamaica with his family.
He isn't going to go with his family.
He's going to go with his girlfriend.

2 Josh and his girlfriend are going to go shopping every day.
______
______

3 Maya is going to stay with her grandparents.
______
______

4 Maya is going to buy a car in September.
______
______

5 Rob and Adele are going to work in a city in Peru.
______
______

6 Rob and Adele are going to help build a hospital.
______
______

☆☆ **4 Complete the next part of the chat show interview with the correct form of *going to*.**

Host When [1] *are you going to make* (make) the *Best of Friends* next series?
Rob We [2] ______ (be) in the studio next January.
Host And [3] ______ you ______ (use) the same writers?
Josh Yes, [4] ______. But they [5] ______ (make) some changes.
Host Really? [6] ______ you ______ (have) new characters?
Maya We can't say at the moment.
Host Okay. What [7] ______ (happen) after Series 2? [8] ______ you ______ (do) other acting jobs?
Josh Yes, I [9] ______.
Maya And Rob and I [10] ______ (try) writing a drama.
Host And you, Adele?
Adele Well, I [11] ______ (not continue) with acting.
Rob What? We didn't know that.
Host But why [12] ______ you ______ (stop)?
Adele I'm [13] ______ (go) back to university.
Maya But that's crazy. You're an actress!
Host Well, that's all we have time for.

5 You have your own chat show. Write questions for your favourite actor. Use *going to* and the words in the box.

- what / do next?
- who / work with?
- when / make / a new film?
- be / on a reality TV show?
- do / some charity work?

1 ______
2 ______
3 ______
4 ______
5 ______

6 Read the information. Complete the email with the correct form of *going to*.

Are you looking for a different holiday?

Come to Poland!

- Fly from London to Kraków and spend two days in this fantastic city.
- Go sightseeing in the Old Town and see the largest medieval square in Europe.
- Visit the famous Wawel Hill and take photos of the wonderful views of the city.
- Spend the rest of your week in Zakopane and enjoy the amazing Tatra Mountains.
- Go walking or mountain biking, or try horse riding in the country.

Hi Donna,
How are you? I'm really excited because I [1] *'m going to go* to Poland with my family soon. We [2] ______ from London to Kraków and we [3] ______ two days there. We [4] ______ in the Old Town. Dad [5] ______ photos of the view of the city from Wawel Hill.
We [6] ______ the rest of the week in Zakopane – a beautiful place in the mountains. Mum and Dad [7] ______ walking in the mountains but my brother and I [8] ______ mountain biking. My sister [9] ______ horse riding in the country.
Email me soon.
Mark

7 Match words from A and B to write questions and true short answers about your next holiday.

A	~~go~~ practise take go stay travel
B	a lot of photos sightseeing ~~abroad~~ your English by car with friends

1 *Are you going to go abroad?*
Yes, I am. OR *No, I'm not.*
2 ______
3 ______
4 ______
5 ______
6 ______

Your Turn

8 Write about plans for your ideal holiday.

I'm going ______ (place) with ______ (people) in ______ (month). We ______ stay ______ (place). I'm going ______ (activity). My ______ (person) ______ (activity) and my ______ (person) ______ (activity).

9 Complete the sentences with true information.

Sentence Builder

1 I'm *going to see my friends* at the weekend.
2 My teacher ______ next week.
3 I ______ tonight.
4 My family and I ______ at the weekend.
5 My mum ______ tomorrow.
6 I ______ this summer.

24 Skills

Vocabulary: Parties

1 Complete the blog with the words in the box.

under-16s club took food danced ~~party~~ holidays invited celebrate DJ group photo

Joe's blog

I went to a great [1] *party* last night. We wanted to [2] ________ the start of the summer [3] ________. We [4] ________ all our school friends! The party was at our [5] ________ from 7 to 11 p.m. We had some great [6] ________ – pizzas, hotdogs and hamburgers. There was a great [7] ________ and he played brilliant music. We [8] ________ for hours. I [9] ________ a lot of photos, too. Here's a brilliant [10] ________ of all my friends.

<< previous post next post >>

Key Expressions: Invitations

2 Complete the dialogue with lines (a–h). There are two lines you don't need.

Sam Hi Liz. How are you?
Liz 1 *h*
Sam I'm going to have a party on Saturday. Would you like to come?
Liz 2 ________
Sam That's great. The party is at my house.
Liz 3 ________
Sam About eight o'clock. Can you bring some music?
Liz 4 ________
Sam Great! Your brother can come to the party, too.
Liz 5 ________
Sam Okay, no problem. See you at the weekend.
Liz 6 ________

a Okay. What time does it start?
b I'd love to, thanks.
c Sorry, I can't.
d Yes! Where's the party?
e Yes, see you then.
f Sorry, he can't. He's going to go to London.
g Sure. You can use my dance CDs.
h ~~Fine, thanks.~~

Listening

28 **3 Listen to Part 1 of the recording. Complete the invitation to Leo's party.**

Invitation

Please come to: 1 *Leo's*
2 ________ birthday party

Date: Saturday, 3 ________ of May

Place: 4 ________ Youth Club

Time: From 5 ________ to 11.00 p.m.

Please bring: some
6 ________

29 **4 Listen to Part 2 of the recording. Tick who can come to Leo's party.**

1 Joe ✓
2 Milly ☐
3 Eddie ☐
4 Helen ☐
5 Paul ☐

Reading

5 Read the invitations (1–4). Match them to the descriptions (a–d).

a note 3
b email
c party invitation
d text message

1

From 00 7960 349

Hi, Jane. R u ok? U want 2 go 2 the cinema 2moro?
luv
Fiona

2

Hi Simon,
Do you want to stay at my house this weekend? Andy is going to be here. He's great fun. We can play computer games and watch football on TV.
Dan

3

Dear Auntie Sue,
We're going to have an art exhibition at my school at the weekend. There's going to be a display of my class's paintings. Would you like to come?
Love, Nick

4

Please come to
Helen's birthday party
On: Sunday 22nd July
From: 2 p.m. to 6 p.m.
At: 22 Palace Road, London
Please reply to: helen@mailme.com
or on 07913 213168

6 Read the invitations again and correct the information.

1 Fiona ~~doesn't want~~ to see a film. *wants*
2 Simon and Andy are going to play football at the weekend. ______
3 Dan is great fun. ______
4 Sue invites Nick to an exhibition. ______
5 Nick is going to go to a museum at the weekend. ______
6 Helen hasn't got an email address. ______

Writing

7 Correct the punctuation in the email. Which invitation in Exercise 5 does it reply to?

hi there
thanks for your invitation Id love to see your pictures – youre a very good artist? uncle John adam and Maria want to come too, what day is it on and what time does it start. can you send me directions please.
see you at the weekend

8 Write a reply to one of the invitations in Exercise 5.

Your Turn

9 Imagine it's your birthday. Write an invitation to a friend. Give this information.

- date
- time
- place
- what to bring

Reading Corner 4

The Battle of Newton Road

1 In Reading Corner 4 there are parts of a story. Look at the title and the picture. What do you think the story is about?

a a competition
b a protest
c a volunteering day

2 Read the description of the story. Check your answer to Exercise 1.

> **The Battle of Newton Road**
> The houses in Newton Road are small but people are very happy there. Then a civil engineer wants to knock down the houses and build a new road. The people of Newton Road are very angry. But can they win the battle?

3 Read about the first part of the story and answer true (T) or false (F).

Sally Robson, Helen Taylor and Paul Johnson are neighbours. They go to a meeting on Saturday March 1st about the new road. Then …

It is Monday. Sally Robson is at school. She tells her students about the meeting. She tells them about Mr Wood and the new road.

'He can't build a new road here,' they say. 'He can't knock down the houses and our school.'

But Mr Wood is a clever man. He shows the new houses to Helen Taylor and Paul Johnson.

'Mr Wood isn't a bad man,' Helen tells Sally. 'And the new houses aren't bad.'

'They're very good,' Paul Johnson says. 'And they have big gardens. Think about that.'

Sally tells them: 'New houses and big gardens aren't important. Friends are important. And a school for your children.'

Stephen and Catherine are two of Sally Robson's students. They go to her house.

'The people want new houses,' Sally Robson tells them. 'We can't win this battle.'

'Yes, we can, Miss Robson,' Stephen says. 'Our friends can help.'

1 Sally is a teacher. ☐
2 The civil engineer's name is Mr Wood. ☐
3 The students aren't worried. ☐
4 Sally's neighbours are interested in the new houses. ☐
5 Sally thinks new houses and big gardens are more important than the community. ☐
6 Stephen, Catherine and their friends aren't going to help Sally. ☐

4 Look at the picture. What do you think happens next? Read the next part of the story and check.

Time passes but the people of Newton Road don't move to the new houses. Then …

June goes and July comes. July goes and August comes. Now Mr Wood isn't very happy.

'I can't wait,' he says. 'It's August. I'm going to build the new road. The people of Newton Road want a battle. They can have a battle!'

On Monday Mr Wood comes to Newton Road. His men are with him. The men have yellow machines. They are big. They can knock down houses.

'I'm going to build the new road,' Mr Wood says.

'No!' Sally Robson says. 'You can't come here with the machines. Look!'

The people of Newton Road are sitting in the road. Stephen and Catherine and their friends from school are sitting with them.

5 Read the text in Exercise 4 again. Choose the correct information.

1 It's *four* / *five* months since the meeting in March.
2 Mr Wood feels *scared of* / *angry* with the people of Newton Road.
3 Mr Wood's men *have* / *haven't* got the equipment to knock down Newton Road.
4 Sally's students *are* / *aren't* part of the protest.

6 Read about the next part of the story. Write the correct names.

Sally has an idea to help the protest. She talks to a newspaper man about the battle of Newton Road. Then …

It's Saturday morning. Stephen and Catherine show the newspaper to Sally Robson. She looks at it.

'THE BATTLE OF NEWTON ROAD,' the newspaper says. 'TEACHER AND STUDENTS IN BATTLE FOR HOMES. CAN THEY SAVE THEIR ROAD?'

'Our photographs are in the newspaper, Miss Robson,' Catherine says. 'Look. We're famous.' …

The people in the town talk about the battle. Some people say: 'Sally Robson and her friends are right. Friends and neighbours are important. Newton Road is their road.'

But some people say: 'Mr Wood is right. We want new roads in this town. The old roads are bad. …'

And some people say: 'Sally Robson is right but Mr Wood is right too. What are they going to do?'

Who / What …

1 speaks to a journalist? ______

2 tells the story of the protest? ______

3 shows Sally their pictures? ______

4 talks about the battle? ______

7 What do you think happens next? Read about the end of the story and check.

It's September. The people of Newton Road have a meeting with Mr Wood at Newton Road School. The headmaster, Mr Morgan, is also there. Then …

'You can have your friends and neighbours,' Mr Wood says, 'but you can have your new houses too. We're going to build new houses in a new road. The road has a new school too. Mr Morgan can be the headmaster. You can stay with your friends. It can be your road.'

'Our road?' the people say.

Mr Wood looks at Sally Robson. 'Robson Road!' he says.

'Robson Road! Yes, good idea!' the people say.

'No!' It's Sally Robson. 'No!' she says. 'It isn't a good idea. … We can stay with our friends in Newton Road. The new Newton Road.'

Mr Wood smiles. 'Yes,' he says. 'It can be the new Newton Road.'

The people of Newton Road smile. 'The new Newton Road,' they say. 'Good idea!'

8 Number the summary of the story in the correct order.

a Mr Woods decides it's time to knock down the houses on Newton Road. ☐
b Sally and her students decide to fight the building of the road. ☐
c There is a meeting in September. ☐
d Mr Wood wants to build a new road. ☐
e Mr Wood and the people agree to build a new Newton Road. ☐
f The people stop the machines from going into the road. ☐
g A journalist writes an article about the protest. ☐

9 Is your road/part of town important to you? Why/Why not?

Language Check 8

Vocabulary

1 Put the letters in order to make TV programmes.

	wesn	n*ews*____
1	ifml	f______
2	oautdrmcnye	d______
3	antoero	c______
4	htea wohs	c______ s______
5	amrda sresie	d______ s______
6	agem hswo	g______ s______
7	rsospt amgrpmore	s______ p______
8	yetlrai ohws	r______ s______
9	osap	s______
10	cumsi roempgrma	m______ p______

☐ / 10

2 Add *-ed* or *-ing* to the adjectives.

*We saw an amaz*ing *programme last night.*

1 I'm not very interest______ in TV. I hardly ever watch it.
2 The film was terrible. We were bor______ from the start.
3 I was amaz______ when I saw the special effects in *Avatar*.
4 This film isn't very interest______ .
5 The match was really bor______ . The teams didn't score.

☐ / 5

Grammar

3 Complete the dialogue with the verbs in the box and *going to*.

~~go~~ go surfing stay buy give work do not go go

A What are your plans for the summer?
B I *'m going to go* on an adventure holiday.
A Wow! Where [1]______ you ______?
B In a hotel in Florida.
A What activities [2]______ you ______?
B I [3]______ – I love the sea! Where [4]______ you ______ for the summer?
A I [5]______ on holiday because I've got a summer job.
B Where [6]______ you ______?
A In my uncle's shop. I [7]______ a new bike and. I [8]______ it to my little brother!

☐ / 8

4 Complete the sentences with the adjectives in the box. Use comparatives or superlatives.

funny good bad difficult boring happy ~~old~~ tall

My grandmother is the oldest *person in my family. She's 85.*

1 You were sad yesterday. Are you ______ today?
2 'Who was the ______ player in the match?' 'Misha, she was brilliant.'
3 'Who is ______, you or your sister?' 'My sister. She's 1m 70cm.'
4 I didn't enjoy the film we saw last night. I thought it was the ______ film of the year.
5 It's raining in the south but the weather is ______ in the rest of the county. It's snowing!
6 I failed Physics. It was a lot ______ than the other exams.
7 I think the ______ actor is Jack Black. I always laugh at his films.

☐ / 7

Key Expressions

5 Choose the correct words.

A (*Would*) / *do* you like [1]*come / to come* to my party on Sunday?
B I'd [2]*love / like* to, thanks.
A [3]*Do / Would* you want to [4]*inviting / invite* your sister?
B Sorry, I [5]*can / can't*. She's going to be in London with her friends.

☐ / 5

What's your score?

Module 8

☐ Vocabulary
☐ Grammar
☐ Key Expressions

☐ / 35

This is easy.
I need more practice.
This is difficult.

Wordlist

Get Ready Unit A

Countries	**/ˈkʌntriz/**
Argentina	/ˌɑːdʒənˈtiːnə/
Australia	/ɒˈstreɪliə/
Brazil	/brəˈzɪl/
Canada	/ˈkænədə/
China	/ˈtʃaɪnə/
Greece	/griːs/
Italy	/ˈɪtəli/
Japan	/dʒəˈpæn/
Poland	/ˈpəʊlənd/
Portugal	/ˈpɔːtʃəgəl/
Russia	/ˈrʌʃə/
Spain	/speɪn/
Turkey	/ˈtɜːki/
the United Kingdom of Great Britain and Northern Ireland	/ðə juːˌnaɪtəd ˈkɪŋdəm əv greɪt ˈbrɪtn ənd ˌnɔːðən ˈaɪələnd/
the United States	/ðə juːˌnaɪtəd ˌsteɪts/

Nationalities	**/ˌnæʃəˈnælətiz/**
American	/əˈmerɪkən/
Argentinian	/ˌɑːdʒənˈtɪniən/
Australian	/ɒˈstreɪliən/
Brazilan	/brəˈzɪliən/
British	/ˈbrɪtɪʃ/
Canadian	/kəˈneɪdiən/
Chinese	/ˌtʃaɪˈniːz/
Greek	/griːk/
Italian	/ɪˈtæliən/
Japanese	/ˌdʒæpəˈniːz/
Polish	/ˈpəʊlɪʃ/
Portuguese	/ˌpɔːtʃəˈgiːz/
Russian	/ˈrʌʃən/
Spanish	/ˈspænɪʃ/
Turkish	/ˈtɜːkɪʃ/

Get Ready Unit B

Numbers	**/ˈnʌmbəz/**
1 one	/wʌn/
2 two	/tuː/
3 three	/θriː/
4 four	/fɔː/
5 five	/faɪv/
6 six	/sɪks/
7 seven	/ˈsevən/
8 eight	/eɪt/
9 nine	/naɪn/
10 ten	/ten/
11 eleven	/ɪˈlevən/
12 twelve	/twelv/
13 thirteen	/ˌθɜːˈtiːn/
14 fourteen	/ˌfɔːˈtiːn/
15 fifteen	/ˌfɪfˈtiːn/
16 sixteen	/ˌsɪkˈstiːn/
17 seventeen	/ˌsevənˈtiːn/
18 eighteen	/ˌeɪˈtiːn/
19 nineteen	/ˌnaɪnˈtiːn/
20 twenty	/ˈtwenti/
30 thirty	/ˈθɜːti/
38 thirty-eight	/ˌθɜːti ˈeɪt/
39 thirty-nine	/ˌθɜːti ˈnaɪn/
40 forty	/ˈfɔːti/
50 fifty	/ˈfɪfti/
60 sixty	/ˈsɪksti/
63 sixty-three	/ˌsɪksti ˈθriː/
65 sixty-five	/ˌsɪksti ˈfaɪv/
70 seventy	/ˈsevənti/
80 eighty	/ˈeɪti/
90 ninety	/ˈnaɪnti/
100 one hundred	/wʌn ˈhʌndrəd/

Family	**/ˈfæməli/**
aunt	/ɑːnt/
brother	/ˈbrʌðə/
child, *pl.* children	/tʃaɪld, ˈtʃɪldrən/
cousin	/ˈkʌzən/
daughter	/ˈdɔːtə/
father	/ˈfɑːðə/
grandfather	/ˈgrændˌfɑːðə/
grandmother	/ˈgrænˌmʌðə/
granddaughter	/ˈgrænˌdɔːtə/
grandparents	/ˈgrænˌpeərənts/
grandson	/ˈgrænsʌn/
husband	/ˈhʌzbənd/
mother	/ˈmʌðə/
nephew	/ˈnefjuː/
niece	/niːs/
parents	/ˈpeərənts/
sister	/ˈsɪstə/
son	/sʌn/
uncle	/ˈʌŋkəl/
wife	/waɪf/

Ordinal Numbers	**/ˌɔːdənəl ˈnʌmbəz/**
first	/fɜːst/
second	/ˈsekənd/
third	/θɜːd/
fourth	/fɔːθ/
fifth	/fɪfθ/
sixth	/sɪksθ/
seventh	/ˈsevənθ/
eighth	/eɪtθ/
ninth	/naɪnθ/
tenth	/tenθ/
eleventh	/ɪˈlevənθ/
twelfth	/twelfθ/
thirteenth	/ˌθɜːˈtiːnθ/
sixteenth	/ˌsɪkˈstiːnθ/
eighteenth	/ˌeɪˈtiːnθ/
twentieth	/ˈtwentiəθ/
twenty-second	/ˌtwenti ˈsekənd/
twenty-third	/ˌtwenti ˈθɜːd/
twenty-sixth	/ˌtwenti ˈsɪksθ/
thirtieth	/ˈθɜːtiəθ/
thirty-first	/ˌθɜːti ˈfɜːst/

Months	**/mʌnθs/**
January	/ˈdʒænjuəri, -njʊri/
February	/ˈfebruəri, ˈfebjʊri/
March	/mɑːtʃ/
April	/ˈeɪprəl/
May	/meɪ/
June	/dʒuːn/
July	/dʒʊˈlaɪ/
August	/ˈɔːgəst/
September	/sepˈtembə/
October	/ɒkˈtəʊbə/
November	/nəʊˈvembə, nə-/
December	/dɪˈsembə/

Get Ready Unit C

Classroom	**/ˈklɑːsruːm, -rʊm/**
bag	/bæg/
bin	/bɪn/
board	/bɔːd/
book	/bʊk/
bookshelf	/ˈbʊkʃelf/
CD player	/ˌsiː ˈdiː ˌpleɪə/
chair	/tʃeə/
computer	/kəmˈpjuːtə
cupboard	/ˈkʌbəd/
desk	/desk/
dictionary	/ˈdɪkʃənəri/
door	/dɔː/
DVD player	/ˌdiː viː ˈdiː ˌpleɪə/
pen	/pen/
pencil	/ˈpensəl/
plant	/plɑːnt/
poster	/ˈpəʊstə/
ruler	/ˈruːlə/
wall	/wɔːl/
watch	/wɒtʃ/
window	/ˈwɪndəʊ/

Get Ready Unit D

School subjects	**/ˈskuːl ˌsʌbdʒɪkts/**
art	/ɑːt/
Chinese	/ˌtʃaɪˈniːz/
English	/ˈɪŋglɪʃ/
geography	/dʒiˈɒgrəfi, ˈdʒɒg-/
history	/ˈhɪstəri/
IT (information technology)	/ˌaɪ ˈtiː, ɪnfəˈmeɪʃən tekˌnɒlədʒi/
maths	/mæθs/
music	/ˈmjuːzɪk/
PE (physical education)	/ˌpiː ˈiː, ˌfɪzɪkəl edjʊˈkeɪʃən/
science	/ˈsaɪəns/

Days of the week	**/ˌdeɪz əv ðə ˈwiːk/**
Monday	/ˈmʌndi, -deɪ/
Tuesday	/ˈtjuːzdi, -deɪ/
Wednesday	/ˈwenzdi, -deɪ/
Thursday	/ˈθɜːzdi, -deɪ/

Friday	/ˈfraɪdi, -deɪ/
Saturday	/ˈsætədi, -deɪ/
Sunday	/ˈsʌndi, -deɪ/

Telling the time	**/ˌtelɪŋ ðə ˈtaɪm/**
What time is …?	/wɒt ˈtaɪm ɪz/
at eight o'clock	/ət ˌeɪt əˈklɒk/
eleven o'clock	/ɪˌlevən əˈklɒk/
five past (three)	/ˌfaɪv pɑːst ˈθriː/
half past (twelve)	/ˌhɑːf pɑːst ˈtwelv/
quarter past (two)	/ˌkwɔːtə pɑːst ˈtuː/
quarter to (twelve)	/ˌkwɔːtə tə ˈtwelv/
ten to (ten)	/ˌten tə ˈten/

Starter Unit E

House	**/haʊs/**
chimney	/ˈtʃɪmni/
downstairs	/ˌdaʊnˈsteəz/
roof	/ruːf/
upstairs	/ˌʌpˈsteəz/

Rooms	**/ruːmz, rʊmz/**
bathroom	/ˈbɑːθrʊm, -ruːm/
bedroom	/ˈbedrʊm, -ruːm/
kitchen	/ˈkɪtʃən/
living room	/ˈlɪvɪŋ ruːm, rʊm/

Furniture and things at home	**/ˈfɜːnɪtʃər ən ˌθɪŋz ət ˈhəʊm/**
armchair	/ˈɑːmtʃeə/
bath	/bɑːθ/
bed	/bed/
carpet	/ˈkɑːpɪt/
CD (compact disc)	/ˌsiː ˈdiː, ˌkɒmpækt ˈdɪsk/
CD player	/ˌsiː ˈdiː ˌpleɪə/
computer	/kəmˈpjuːtə/
cooker	/ˈkʊkə/
curtains	/ˈkɜːtənz/
desk	/desk/
fireplace	/ˈfaɪəpleɪs/
floor	/flɔː/
fridge	/frɪdʒ/
lamp	/læmp/
magazine	/ˌmægəˈziːn/
microwave	/ˈmaɪkrəweɪv/
mirror	/ˈmɪrə/
poster	/ˈpəʊstə/
shower	/ˈʃaʊə/
sink	/sɪŋk/
sofa	/ˈsəʊfə/
table	/ˈteɪbəl/
television	/ˈteləˌvɪʒən, ˌteləˈvɪʒən/
toilet	/ˈtɔɪlət/
wardrobe	/ˈwɔːdrəʊb/
washbasin	/ˈwɒʃˌbeɪsən/
washing machine	/ˈwɒʃɪŋ məˌʃiːn/

Colours	**/ˈkʌləz/**
black	/blæk/
blue	/bluː/
brown	/braʊn/
green	/griːn/
grey	/greɪ/
orange	/ˈɒrəndʒ/
pink	/pɪŋk/
purple	/ˈpɜːpəl/
red	/red/
white	/waɪt/
yellow	/ˈjeləʊ/

Starter Unit F

Parts of the body	**/ˌpɑːts əv ðə ˈbɒdi/**
arm	/ɑːm/
back	/bæk/
ear	/ɪə/
elbow	/ˈelbəʊ/
finger	/ˈfɪŋgə/
foot, *pl.* feet	/fʊt, fiːt/
hand	/hænd/
head	/hed/
knee	/niː/
leg	/leg/
mouth	/maʊð/
neck	/nek/
nose	/nəʊz/
toe	/təʊ/

Adjectives	**/ˈædʒɪktɪvz/**
big	/bɪg/
blond	/blɒnd/
dark	/dɑːk/
fat	/fæt/
old	/əʊld/
short	/ʃɔːt/
small	/smɔːl/
tall	/tɔːl/
thin	/θɪn/
young	/jʌŋ/

Module 1 – Get Ready

Interests	**/ˈɪntrəsts/**
chess	/tʃes/
computers	/kəmˈpjuːtəz/
computer games	/kəmˈpjuːtə geɪmz/
cycling	/ˈsaɪklɪŋ/
fashion	/ˈfæʃən/
films	/fɪlmz/
horse riding	/ˈhːɔs ˌraɪdɪŋ/
music	/ˈmjuːzɪk/
photography	/fəˈtɒgrəfi/
pottery	/ˈpɒtəri/
reading	/ˈriːdɪŋ/
singing	/ˈsɪŋɪŋ/
swimming	/ˈswɪmɪŋ/

Module 1 – Unit 1

Abilities	**/əˈbɪlətiz/**
act	/ækt/
cook	/kʊk/
dance	/dɑːns/
draw	/drɔː/
paint	/peɪnt/
play a musical instrument	/ˌpleɪ ə ˌmjuːzɪkəl ˈɪnstrəmənt/
play the guitar	/ˌpleɪ ðə gɪˈtɑː/
play the piano	/ˌpleɪ ðə piˈænəʊ/
play the violin	/ˌpleɪ ðə vaɪəˈlɪn/
play chess	/ˌpleɪ ˈtʃes/
ride a bike	/ˌraɪd ə ˈbaɪk/
sing	/sɪŋ/
speak Chinese	/ˌspiːk tʃaɪˈniːz/
take photos	/ˌteɪk ˈfəʊtəʊz/
use a computer	/ˌjuːz ə kəmˈpjuːtə/
write stories	/ˌraɪt ˈstɔːriz/

Module 1 – Unit 3

Opinion adjectives	**/əˈpɪnjən ˌædʒɪktɪvz/**
boring	/ˈbɔːrɪŋ/
brilliant	/ˈbrɪljənt/
cool	/kuːl/
great	/greɪt/
interesting	/ˈɪntrəstɪŋ/
nice	/naɪs/
not bad	/ˌnɒt ˈbæd/
okay	/ˌəʊˈkeɪ/
pretty	/ˈprɪti/
silly	/ˈsɪli/

Module 2 – Get Ready

Sport and exercise	**/ˌspɔːt ən ˈeksəsaɪz/**
athletics	/æθˈletɪks, əθ-/
badminton	/ˈbædmɪntən/
basketball	/ˈbɑːskɪtbɔːl/
cycling	/ˈsaɪklɪŋ/
football	/ˈfʊtbɔːl/
gymnastics	/dʒɪmˈnæstɪks/
hockey	/ˈhɒki/
horse riding	/ˈhɔːs ˌraɪdɪŋ/
ice skating	/ˈaɪs ˌskeɪtɪŋ/
judo	/ˈdʒuːdəʊ/
rugby	/ˈrʌgbi/
running	/ˈrʌnɪŋ/
skateboarding	/ˈskeɪtbɔːdɪŋ/
surfing	/ˈsɜːfɪŋ/
swimming	/ˈswɪmɪŋ/
tennis	/ˈtenɪs/
volleyball	/ˈvɒlibɔːl/
walking	/ˈwɔːkɪŋ/

Module 2 – Unit 4

Appearance	**/əˈpɪərəns/**
beard	/bɪəd/
black hair	/ˌblæk ˈheə/
blond hair	/ˌblɒnd ˈheə/
blue eyes	/ˌbluː ˈaɪz/
brown eyes	/ˌbraʊn ˈaɪz/
curly hair	/ˌkɜːli ˈheə/
dark hair	/ˌdɑːk ˈheə/
earring	/ˈɪərɪŋ/
fair hair	/ˌfeə ˈheə/
fat	/fæt/
green eyes	/ˌgriːn ˈaɪz/
long hair	/ˌlɒŋ ˈheə/
medium-length hair	/ˌmiːdiəm leŋθ ˈheə/

ponytail	/ˈpəʊniteɪl/
red hair	/ˌred ˈheə/
shaved head	/ˌʃeɪvd ˈhed/
short hair	/ˌʃɔ:t ˈheə/
slim	/slɪm/
straight hair	/ˌstreɪt ˈheə/
thin	/θɪn/
tattoo	/təˈtu:, tæˈtu:/
Clothes	**/kləʊðz, kləʊz/**
boots	/bu:ts/
cap	/kæp/
coat	/kəʊt/
dress	/dres/
hat	/hæt/
jacket	/ˈdʒækɪt/
jeans	/dʒi:nz/
shirt	/ʃɜ:t/
shoes	/ʃu:z/
shorts	/ʃɔ:ts/
skirt	/skɜ:t/
socks	/sɒks/
tracksuit	/ˈtræksu:t, -sju:t/
trainers	/ˈtreɪnəz/
trousers	/ˈtraʊzəz/
T-shirt	/ˈti: ʃɜ:t/

Module 2 – Unit 5

Food and drink	**/ˌfu:d ən ˈdrɪŋk/**
apple	/ˈæpəl/
banana	/bəˈnɑ:nə/
beans	/bi:nz/
biscuits	/ˈbɪskɪts/
bottle of (water)	/ˌbɒtl əv ˈwɔ:tə/
bread	/bred/
can of (cola)	/ˌkæn əv ˈkəʊlə/
carrot	/ˈkærət/
carton of (orange juice)	/ˌkɑ:tn əv ˈɒrəndʒ dʒu:s/
cereal	/ˈsɪəriəl/
cheese	/tʃi:z/
chicken	/ˈtʃɪkən/
chips	/tʃɪps/
coffee	/ˈkɒfi/
crisps	/krɪsps/
egg	/eg/
fish	/fɪʃ/
fruit	/fru:t/
hamburger	/ˈhæmbɜ:gə/
hot dog	/ˈhɒt dɒg/
ice cream	/ˌaɪs ˈkri:m/
kiwi	/ˈki:wi:/
lemon	/ˈlemən/
melon	/ˈmelən/
meat	/mi:t/
milk	/mɪlk/
nuts	/nʌts/
orange	/ˈɒrəndʒ/
packet of (crisps)	/ˌpækət əv ˈkrɪsps/
pasta	/ˈpæstə/
peanuts	/ˈpi:nʌts/
pizza	/ˈpi:tsə/
potato	/pəˈteɪtəʊ/
rice	/raɪs/
salad	/ˈsæləd/
sandwich	/ˈsænwɪdʒ/
steak	/steɪk/
sweet	/swi:t/
tea	/ti:/
toast	/təʊst/
tomato	/təˈmɑ:təʊ/
vegetable	/ˈvedʒtəbəl/
water	/ˈwɔ:tə/

Module 3 – Get Ready

Jobs	**/dʒɒbz/**
actor/actress	/ˈæktə, ˈæktrəs/
builder	/ˈbɪldə/
cook	/kʊk/
dentist	/ˈdentəst/
doctor	/ˈdɒktə/
electrician	/ɪˌlekˈtrɪʃən, ˌelɪk-/
farmer	/ˈfɑ:mə/
fire fighter	/ˈfaɪə ˌfaɪtə/
footballer	/ˈfʊtbɔ:lə/
football manager	/ˈfʊtbɔ:l ˌmænɪdʒə/
journalist	/ˈdʒɜ:nəlɪst/
mechanic	/mɪˈkænɪk/
model	/ˈmɒdl/
nurse	/nɜ:s/
pilot	/ˈpaɪlət/
police officer	/pəˈli:s ˌɒfɪsə/
racing driver	/ˈreɪsɪŋ ˌdraɪvə/
scientist	/ˈsaɪəntɪst/
secretary	/ˈsekrətəri/
singer	/ˈsɪŋə/
teacher	/ˈti:tʃə/
tennis player	/ˈtenɪs ˌpleɪə/
vet	/vet/
waiter/waitress	/ˈweɪtə, ˈweɪtrəs/
window cleaner	/ˈwɪndəʊ ˌkli:nə/
Adjectives	**/ˈædʒɪktɪvz/**
boring	/ˈbɔ:rɪŋ/
dangerous	/ˈdeɪndʒərəs/
difficult	/ˈdɪfɪkəlt/
easy	/ˈi:zi/
interesting	/ˈɪntrəstɪŋ/
safe	/seɪf/

Module 3 – Unit 7

Daily routines	**/ˌdeɪli ru:ˈti:nz/**
brush your teeth	/ˌbrʌʃ jə ˈti:θ/
do the dishes	/ˌdu: ðə ˈdɪʃəz/
do some exercise	/ˌdu: səm ˈeksəsaɪz/
do your homework	/ˌdu: jə ˈhəʊmwɜ:k/
do the housework	/ˌdu: ðə ˈhaʊswɜ:k/
empty the rubbish bins	/ˌempti ðə ˈrʌbɪʃ bɪnz/
get up	/get ˈʌp/
go shopping	/ˌgəʊ ˈʃɒpɪŋ/
go to bed	/ˌgəʊ tə ˈbed/
have a shower	/hæv ə ˈʃaʊə/
have breakfast/ lunch/dinner	/hæv ˈbrekfəst, ˈlʌntʃ, ˈdɪnə/
make your bed	/ˌmeɪk jə ˈbed/
play cards/chess	/ˌpleɪ ˈkɑ:dz, ˈtʃes/
tidy your room	/ˌtaɪdi jə ˈru:m, ˈrʊm/
wash your clothes	/ˌwɒʃ jə ˈkləʊðz, ˈkləʊz/
watch TV	/ˌwɒtʃ ti: ˈvi:/

Module 3 – Unit 8

The Internet	**/ði ˈɪntənet/**
delete a file/ an email/ an attachment	/dɪˌli:t ə ˈfaɪl, ən ˈi:meɪl, ən əˈtætʃmənt/
download music/ a file/a photo	/ˌdaʊnləʊd ˈmju:zɪk, ə ˈfaɪl, ə ˈfəʊtəʊ/
receive an email/ an attachment	/rɪˌsi:v ən ˈi:meɪl, ən əˈtætʃmənt/
save a file/ an email/ an attachment	/ˌseɪv ə ˈfaɪl, ən ˈi:meɪl, ən əˈtætʃmənt/
chat online	/ˌtʃæt ɒnˈlaɪn/
use a password/ a nickname	/ˌju:z ə ˈpɑ:swɜ:d, ə ˈnɪkneɪm/

Module 3 – Unit 9

Feelings	**/ˈfi:lɪŋz/**
bored	/bɔ:d/
excited	/ɪkˈsaɪtəd/
happy	/ˈhæpi/
hungry	/ˈhʌŋgri/
nervous	/ˈnɜ:vəs/
relaxed	/rɪˈlækst/
scared	/skeəd/
sick	/sɪk/
tired	/taɪəd/
unhappy	/ʌnˈhæpi/
worried	/ˈwʌrid/

Module 4 – Get Ready

Places	**/ˈpleɪsɪz/**
amusement park	/əˈmju:zmənt pɑ:k/
bowling alley	/ˈbəʊlɪŋ ˌæli/
cinema	/ˈsɪnəmə/
coffee bar	/ˈkɒfi bɑ:/
disco	/ˈdɪskəʊ/
ice rink	/ˈaɪs rɪŋk/
Internet café	/ˌɪntənet ˈkæfeɪ/
library	/ˈlaɪbrəri, -bri/
museum	/mju:ˈziəm/
shop	/ʃɒp/
shopping centre	/ˈʃɒpɪŋ ˌsentə/
skatepark	/ˈskeɪtpɑ:k/
snack bar	/ˈsnæk bɑ:/
sports centre	/ˈspɔ:ts ˌsentə/
swimming pool	/ˈswɪmɪŋ pu:l/
under-16s' club	/ˌʌndə sɪkˈsti:nz klʌb/
water park	/ˈwɔ:tə pɑ:k/
zoo	/zu:/

Module 4 – Unit 12

Places	**/ˈpleɪsəz/**
bank	/bæŋk/
car park	/ˈkɑː pɑːk/
church	/tʃɜːtʃ/
hospital	/ˈhɒspɪtl/
hotel	/həʊtel/
park	/pɑːk/
police station	/pəˈliːs ˌsteɪʃən/
post office	/ˈpəʊst ˌɒfɪs/
railway station	/ˈreɪlweɪ ˌsteɪʃən/
river	/ˈrɪvə/
theatre	/ˈθɪətə/
tourist information	/ˌtʊərɪst ɪnfəˈmeɪʃən/

Directions	**/dəˈrekʃənz, daɪ-/**
cross	/krɒs/
go down	/gəʊ ˈdaʊn/
go out of	/gəʊ ˈaʊt əv, ɒv/
go past	/gəʊ ˈpɑːst/
on the corner	/ɒn ðə ˈkɔːnə/
on the left/right	/ɒn ðə ˈleft, ˈraɪt/
opposite	/ˈɒpəzɪt/
turn right/left	/ˌtɜːn ˈraɪt, ˈleft/

Compass points	**/ˈkʌmpəs pɔɪnts/**
east	/iːst/
north	/nɔːθ/
north east	/ˌnɔːθ ˈiːst/
north west	/ˌnɔːθ ˈwest/
south	/saʊθ/
south east	/ˌsaʊθ ˈiːst/
south west	/ˌsaʊθ ˈwest/
west	/west/

Module 5 – Get Ready

The Weather – Adjectives	**/ðə ˈweðə ˌˈædʒɪktɪvz/**
cloudy	/ˈklaʊdi/
cold	/kəʊld/
foggy	/ˈfɒgi/
hot	/hɒt/
icy	/ˈaɪsi/
rainy	/ˈreɪni/
snowy	/ˈsnəʊi/
sunny	/ˈsʌni/
warm	/wɔːm/
wet	/wet/
windy	/ˈwɪndi/
What's the weather like today?	/ˌwɒts ðə ˈweðə laɪk təˌdeɪ/

Module 5 – Unit 13

The Weather – Nouns	**/ðə ˈweðə/ /naʊnz/**
cloud	/klaʊd/
fog	/fɒg/
rain	/reɪn/
snow	/snəʊ/
sun	/sʌn/
wind	/wɪnd/

Seasons	**/ˈsiːzənz/**
autumn	/ˈɔːtəm/
spring	/sprɪŋ/
summer	/ˈsʌmə/
winter	/ˈwɪntə/

Module 6 – Get Ready

Transport	**/ˈtrænspɔːt/**
balloon	/bəˈluːn/
bike (bicycle)	/baɪk, ˈbaɪsɪkəl/
boat	/bəʊt/
bus	/bʌs/
camel	/ˈkæməl/
canoe	/kəˈnuː/
car	/kɑː/
ferry	/ˈferi/
helicopter	/ˈhelɪkɒptə/
horse	/hɔːs/
plane	/pleɪn/
rocket	/ˈrɒkət/
ship	/ʃɪp/
sledge	/sledʒ/
train	/treɪn/

Module 6 – Unit 16

Space	**/speɪs/**
astronaut	/ˈæstrənɔːt/
crew	/kruː/
Earth	/ɜːθ/
equipment	/ɪˈkwɪpmənt/
experiment	/ɪkˈsperəmənt/
mission	/ˈmɪʃən/
moon	/muːn/
oxygen	/ˈɒksɪdʒən/
planet	/ˈplænət/
space station	/ˈspeɪs ˌsteɪʃən/

Module 7 – Get Ready

Helping	**/ˈhelpɪŋ/**
help animals/ the environment/ the community	/ˌhelp ˈænəməlz, ði ɪnˈvaɪrənmənt, ðə kəˈmjuːnəti/
recycle batteries/ bottles/paper/ plastic/tins	/riːˌsaɪkəl ˈbætəriz, ˈbɒtlz, ˈpeɪpə, ˈplæstɪk, ˈtɪnz/
save electricity/ water	/ˌseɪv elɪkˈtrɪsəti, ˈwɔːtə/
turn off the lights/ the taps/the TV/ the computer	/ˌtɜːn ɒf ðə ˈlaɪts, ðə ˈtæps, ðə ˌtiː ˈviː, ðə kəmˈpjuːtə/

Module 7 – Unit 19

Animals	**/ˈænəməlz/**
American bald eagle	/əˌmerɪkən ˌbɔːld ˈiːgəl/
Amur tiger	/ˌæmʊə ˈtaɪgə/
bear	/beə/
bird	/bɜːd/
black rhino	/ˌblæk ˈraɪnəʊ/
blue whale	/ˌbluː ˈweɪl/
buffalo	/ˈbʌfələʊ/
butterfly	/ˈbʌtəflaɪ/
camel	/ˈkæməl/
cat	/kæt/
cheetah	/ˈtʃiːtə/
cow	/kaʊ/
crocodile	/ˈkrɒkədaɪl/
dog	/dɒg/
dolphin	/ˈdɒlfin/
duck	/dʌk/
elephant	/ˈeləfənt/
falcon	/ˈfɔːlkən/
fish	/fɪʃ/
fox	/fɒks/
frog	/frɒg/
giraffe	/dʒəˈrɑːf/
goat	/gəʊt/
gorilla	/gəˈrɪlə/
hen	/hen/
hippopotamus (hippo)	/ˌhɪpəˈpɒtəməs, ˈhɪpəʊ/
horse	/hɔːs/
iguana	/ɪˈgwɑːnə/
irrawady dolphin	/ˌɪrəwɒdi ˈdɒlfɪn/
koala	/kəʊˈɑːlə/
komodo dragon	/kəˌməʊdəʊ ˈdrægən/
lion	/ˈlaɪən/
lizard	/ˈlɪzəd/
monkey	/ˈmʌŋki/
ostrich	/ˈɒstrɪtʃ/
panda	/ˈpændə/
parrot	/ˈpærət/
penguin	/ˈpeŋgwɪn/
pig	/pɪg/
polar bear	/ˌpəʊlə ˈbeə/
rabbit	/ˈræbɪt/
seal	/siːl/
shark	/ʃɑːk/
sheep	/ʃiːp/
sloth	/sləʊθ/
snake	/sneɪk/
tiger	/ˈtaɪgə/
tortoise	/ˈtɔːtəs/
whale	/weɪl/
wolf	/wʊlf/

Module 8 – Get Ready

TV programmes	**/ˌtiː ˈviː ˌprəʊgræmz/**
cartoon	/kɑːˈtuːn/
chat show	/ˈtʃæt ʃəʊ/
documentary	/ˌdɒkjəˈmentəri/
drama series	/ˈdrɑːmə ˌsɪəriːz/
film	/fɪlm/
game show	/ˈgeɪm ʃəʊ/
music programme	/ˈmjuːzɪk ˌprəʊgræm/
news	/njuːz/
reality show	/riˈæləti ʃəʊ/
sitcom	/ˈsɪtkɒm/
soap	/səʊp/
sports programme	/ˈspɔːts ˌprəʊgræm/

to be → Get Ready A, page 3

Use

- Look at the examples of *to be* in the present tense:

My name's Amy.
***I'm** sixteen.*
*We**'re** French.*
*Where **are** you from?*
*She **isn't** at school.*
***Are** they at home? No, they **aren't**.*

Form

Affirmative		
I He/She/It We/You/They	**'m** (am) **'s** (is) **'re** (are)	Polish.
Negative		
I He/She/It We/You/They	**'m not** (am not) **isn't** (is not) **aren't** (are not)	from Spain.

***Yes/No* questions**			**Short answers**	
Am **Is** **Are**	I he/she/it we/you/they	late?	Yes, I **am**. Yes, he/she/it **is**. Yes, we/you/they **are**.	No, **I'm not**. No, he/she/it **isn't**. No, we/you/they **aren't**.

Wh- questions
What**'s** your name? Where **are** they from?

1 Complete the sentences with the correct form of *to be*. Use short forms where possible.

1 My name's Jelena and I ________ from Zagreb, in Croatia.
2 My best friends ________ Miguel and Victor. They ________ from Argentina.
3 I ________ from Turkey, but my teacher ________ . She ________ from the United States.
4 We ________ students. We ________ from Turkey.
5 My friends and I ________ in London, but we ________ English, we ________ Irish.
6 Carlos ________ a student. He ________ in Madrid, but he ________ Spanish. He ________ from Mexico.

2 Write questions and answers.

1 where / you / from? (Cintra, in Portugal)
Where are you from?
I'm from Cintra, in Portugal.
2 your / friends / Polish? (no)
____
____
3 what / nationality / your teacher? (he / Canadian)
____
____
4 what / your / name? (Pablo)
____
____
5 your teacher / from / England? (no / he)
____
____
6 Eva / a student? (yes / she)
____
____

Possessive adjectives/'s → Get Ready B, page 5

Use

- We use possessive adjectives in front of nouns:

***My** sister is 19.*
*That's **our** house.*

- We use -*'s* and -*s'* to talk about possessions:

*Is this Peter**'s** jacket?*
*These are my friends**'** CDs.*

Form

Possessive adjectives
my your his her its our your their

-'s / -s'		
Singular noun	+ 's	teacher**'s**
Singular noun ending in *s*	+ 's	Charles**'s**
Regular plural noun	+ *s'*	teams**'**
Irregular plural noun	+ 's	men**'s**, people**'s**, children**'s**, women**'s**

1 Choose the correct words.

1 Is this *you* / *your* bag?
2 *My* / *I* sisters are both teachers.
3 This isn't Dad's phone. *Her* / *His* mobile is black.
4 I've got two brothers. *Their* / *Theirs* names are Pedro and Luis.
5 This is our dog. *It's* / *Its* name is Rocky.
6 I've got one sister. *Her* / *His* name is Liz.
7 *Ours* / *Our* new teachers are very nice.

2 Add *'s* or *s'* to the underlined words.

1 My grandparents' names are Raquel and Diego.
2 Serena Williams sister is Venus Williams.
3 Ana favourite food is chicken.
4 We are students at a girl school.
5 A lot of people favourite sport is football.
6 The new student name is David.
7 The tennis player families are at the match.
8 Where are mum keys?

Plural nouns → Get Ready C, page 6

Word Builder

- Most nouns add *s*:
chair — chairs *girl — girls*
magazine — magazines
- Nouns ending in *x*, *ch*, *s*, and *sh* add *es*:
box — boxes *watch — watches*
class — classes *brush — brushes*
- Nouns ending in a consonant and *y*, change *y* to *ies*:
dictionary — dictionaries *city — cities*
- Most nouns ending in *f* or *fe*, change *f*/*fe* to *ves*:
bookshelf — bookshelves *wife — wives*
- Some plural nouns are irregular:
*person — **people*** *man — **men***
*woman — **women*** *child — **children***
*mouse — **mice*** *sheep — **sheep***
*fish — **fish***

Complete the sentences with the plural form of the words in the box.

~~student~~ city man child dictionary bookshelf person box

1 All the *students* in my school are Spanish.
2 Madrid and Barcelona are ______ in Spain.
3 Check the spelling in your ______ .
4 The CDs are on my ______ .
5 How many ______ are there in your town?
6 Please put the ______ of books in the cupboard.
7 My brothers are the only ______ in my family.
8 They're married but they haven't got any ______ .

Prepositions of place → Get Ready C, page 6

- We use prepositions of place (*in*, *on*, *under*, etc.) to say where things are:
*There's a CD **on** the desk.*
*Is the cat **under** the table?*
*Who's **in** the kitchen?*
*My house is **next to** the park.*
*The supermarket is **between** the library and the bank.*

Look at the picture. Complete the sentences with the correct preposition of place.

1 The CDs are *on* the floor.
2 The desk is ______ the bed.
3 The chair are ______ the desk.
4 The objects are ______ the bedroom.
5 The computer is ______ the bookshelf.
6 The chair is ______ the CDs.
7 The bed is ______ the window and the desk.
8 The CD player is ______ the shelf.

Imperatives → Get Ready D, page 8

Use

- We use the imperative to give people instructions. Remember to use *please* to make the instruction sound polite:
Pass me the dictionary, please.
Don't talk, please.

Form

The imperative is the infinitive without *to*.

Affirmative	Negative
Open your books.	**Don't talk** to your partner.

Write the words in the correct order. Add the correct punctuation.

1 the / please / open / window
Open the window, please.
2 the / exam / use / don't / please / a / in / calculator
______
3 mobile / me / pass / please / my / phone
______
4 please / next / sit / me / to
______
5 book / your / look / don't / at / partner's
______
6 class / for / be / don't / next / late / the
______

Object pronouns → Get Ready D, page 8

Use

- We use subject pronouns
– in front of verbs, e.g. ***I** am a doctor.*
– so that we don't repeat a noun,
e.g. *My brother is 21. **He's** at university.*
- We use object pronouns to replace nouns:
*Read the words and copy **them**.*

Form

Subject pronouns	Object pronouns
I	me
you	you
he	him
she	her
it	it
we	us
you	you
they	them

Choose the correct words.

1 Please tell *we* / (*us*) the right answer.
2 Sit here next to *I* / *me*.
3 Read the sentences and copy *it* / *them*.
4 Susana is a student. *Her's* / *She's* from Spain.
5 *We* / *Us* are from Adelaide, in Australia.
6 This book is for my brother. Please give it to *her* / *him*.
7 Look at the dialogue. Read *it* / *his* in pairs.
8 Where are *them* / *they* from? Cork, in Ireland.

this, that, these, those → Get Ready E, page 9

Use

- We use *this* and *these* to talk about people or things that are close to us:
***This** is my classroom.*
***These** are my friends.*
- We use *that* and *those* for people or things that are further away from us:
***That** man is my teacher.*
***Those** T-shirts are nice.*

Form

- We use *this* and *that* with singular nouns:
***This** CD is my favourite.*
***That's** a poster from a concert.*
- We use *these* and *those* with plural nouns:
***These** are my computer games.*
***Those** are sports games.*

Complete the sentences with *this*, *that*, *these*, *those*.

1 ___*This*___ is Angela. She's my best friend.
2 Come over here and look at ______ photo.
3 ______ lady over there is Mrs Clarke.
4 Look at ______ animals over here.
5 Are ______ your CDs on the desk over there?
6 Is ______ Elena in the car over there?

Articles → Get Ready F, page 10

- We use *a* and *an* with singular nouns
– to talk about a person's job:
*He's **a** fire fighter.*
– when we talk about one of many people or things (compare *the*, below):
*We've got **a** garden.*
- We use *a* before a consonant sound. We use *an* before a vowel sound:
*You've got **a** motorbike.*
*I've got **an** MP3 player.*
- We use *the* with singular nouns and plural nouns
– when we talk about one particular person or thing:
*My mother is in **the** garden. (= the garden of my house)*
– when we talk about a particular group:
*Look at **the** pictures on page 10.*

Choose the correct words.

1 Lucia is *a* / *an* / (*the*) captain of the basketball team.
2 Mark is *a* / *an* / *the* American student.
3 That's *a* / *an* / *the* old photo of my grandmother.
4 **A** Where's dad?
  B He's in *a* / *an* / *the* garden.
5 Mr King is *a* / *an* / *the* good teacher.
6 Put *a* / *an* / *the* boxes in the cupboard, please.

can (ability) → Unit 1, page 12

Use

- We use ***can*/*can't*** + infinitive without *to* to talk about abilities:
*I **can play** the piano but I **can't dance**.*

Form

Affirmative				
I/You/He/She/It/We/They			**can**	swim.
Negative				
I/You/He/She/It/We/They			**can't** (cannot)	swim.
***Yes/No* questions**			**Short answers**	
Can	I/you/he/she/it/we/they	swim?	Yes, I/you/he/she/it/we/they **can**.	No, I/you/he/she/it/we/they **can't**.
***Wh-* questions**				
What can you do?				

1 Write sentences. Use the correct form of *can* and *but*.

1 I / swim (✓) / surf (✗)
I can swim but I can't surf.
2 Barbara / act (✓) / sing (✗)
3 My mum / use a computer (✓) / play computer games (✗)
4 We / draw (✓) / write stories (✗)
5 Enrique / paint (✓) / play the guitar (✗)
6 My sisters / dance (✓) / ice skate (✗)

2 Write questions and short answers.

1 you / swim? (yes)
Can you swim?
Yes, I can.
2 you and your friends / speak English? (yes)
3 your dad / speak French? (no)
4 your sister / play the piano? (yes)
5 your brothers / play tennis? (no)
6 you / ride a horse? (no)

Question words → Unit 2, page 15

- Look at these examples with question words:

Age: ***How old** are you?*
Things: ***What** languages can you speak?*
Place: ***Where** are they from?*
People: ***Who** is your teacher?*
A number: ***How many** brothers and sisters have you got?*
Feelings: ***How** are things?*
Time: ***When** do you go on holiday?*
Frequency: ***How often** do you go out?*
Reason: ***Why** are you late?*
Possession: ***Whose** car is that?*

Write questions for the answers.

1 *What's your name?*
My name's Yasemin.
2
We're from Manchester.
3
I'm 20 years old.
4
Two – Polish and English.
5
I can play the guitar and the piano.
6
My favourite actor is Johnny Depp.

have got / has got → Unit 4, page 21

Use

- We use have got

– to talk about possessions:
*He's **got** a mobile phone.*
*She **hasn't got** a computer.*
– to talk about a person's family:
*I've **got** a brother and a sister.*
– to talk about the appearance of people and things:
*David's **got** dark hair.*
*The museum **has got** five floors.*

Form

Affirmative					
I/You/We/They He/She/It	**'ve got** (have got) **'s got** (has got)	blue eyes.			
Negative					
I/You/We/They He/She/It	**haven't got** (have not got) **hasn't got** (has not got)	a computer.			
***Yes/No* questions**				**Short answers**	
Have	I/you/we/they	**got**	a tattoo?	Yes, I/you/we/they **have**.	No, I/you/we/they **haven't**.
Has	he/she/it	**got**	dark hair?	Yes, he/she/it **has**.	No, he/she/it **hasn't**.
***Wh-* questions**					
What	**have** **has**		I/you/we/they he/she/it		**got?** **got?**

Complete the interview with the correct form of *have got*.

A Can I ask you some questions about technology?
B Yes, okay.
A [1] *Have* you and your family *got* a computer?
B Yes, we [2]________ . We [3]________ two computers. My mum and dad [4]________ one and I [5]________ one in my bedroom.
A Okay. And [6]________ you ________ a printer?
B Yes, we [7]________ .
A And what about mobile phones?
B I [8]________ a mobile and all my friends [9]________ one, too. But my sister [10]________ a mobile because she's only two years old.

Countable/uncountable nouns, *some* and *any* → Unit 5, page 22

- Many nouns in English are countable. We can count them:
*a glass — **100 glasses***
*an orange — **two oranges***
- Some nouns in English are uncountable. We can't count these things. We can't say 'two waters, three moneys'.
- We use *a*/*an* with singular countable nouns:
*I've got **a** cake for you.*
- We use *some* or a number with plural countable nouns in affirmative sentences:
*Buy **some** biscuits from town.*
*We've got **four** nice cakes.*
- We also use *some* with uncountable nouns in affirmative sentences:
*We've got **some** water for you.*
- We use *any* with plural countable and uncountable nouns in negative sentences and in questions:
***Don't eat any** sweets before lunch.*
*We **haven't got any** money.*
***Has** he **got any** crisps?*
***Have** you **got any** homework?*

Correct the underlined mistakes.

1 Here, have <u>some</u> apple. *an*
2 We haven't got any <u>biscuit</u>. ______
3 Is that your <u>moneys</u> on the table? ______
4 Have you got <u>a</u> water in that bottle? ______
5 We've got <u>any</u> nice food for lunch. ______
6 You've got <u>a</u> great new trainers. ______
7 Have you got <u>a</u> new DVDs? ______
8 We haven't got <u>a</u> homework today. ______

Present Simple → Unit 7, page 30,31; Unit 8, page 33

Use

- We use the Present Simple to talk about routines and habits, or something that is true in general:
*I **work** in a hospital.*
*My mum **doesn't like** rap.*
- We often use the Present Simple with time expressions with *at*, *on* and *in*:
*I **get up at** seven o'clock.*
*He **watches** television **at** weekends.*
***Do** you **go out on** Fridays?*
*What **does** he **do in** the morning? (… afternoon?, … evening?)*
- We also use the Present Simple with expressions with *every*:
*I **play** sport **every** week.*
***Do** you **watch** TV **every** day?*

Form

Affirmative					
I/You/We/They He/She/It		**work** **works***	in a school.		
Negative					
I/You/We/They He/She/It	**don't** (do not) **doesn't** (does not)		**work** **work**	in a hospital.	
***Yes/No* questions**			**Short answers**		
Do	I/you/we/they	need a computer?	Yes, I/you/we/they **do**.	No, I/you/we/they **don't**.	
Does	he/she/it	live near here?	Yes, he/she/it **does**.	No, he/she/it **doesn't**.	
***Wh-* questions**					
What	**do**	I/you/we/they	need?		
Where	**does**	he/she/it	go?		

* Spelling of he/she/it forms:

Most verbs	+ *s*	*use*	*uses*
do, *go* and verbs ending in *ch*, *sh*, *s* and *x*	+ *es*	*do* *watch*	*does* *watches*
Verbs ending in consonant + *y*	change *y* to *i* and + *es*	*study*	***studies***
Verbs ending in vowel + *y*	+ *s*	*play*	*plays*
have	*has*	*have*	***has***

1 Complete the text with the correct form of the verb in brackets.

My mum is a nurse at the local hospital but she [1] *doesn't work* (not work) in the morning or afternoon. She [2] ______ (work) in the evening. She [3] ______ (finish) work at 2 a.m. She [4] ______ (get up) late in the morning. My sister and I [5] ______ (not see) her. Our dad [6] ______ (drive) us and then he [7] ______ (go) to work at his office. We all [8] ______ (have) dinner together in the evening.

2 Write questions and short answers.

1 you / do judo? (no)
Do you do judo?
No, I don't.

2 your dad / play golf? (yes)
______
______

3 you / ride a bike to school? (no)
______
______

4 your mum and dad / play sport? (yes)
______
______

5 your brother / study English? (no)
______
______

6 your grandmother / use the Internet? (yes)
______
______

Adverbs → Unit 10, page 38

- These are adverbs of frequency:

0% ⟵⟶ 100%

never *hardly ever* *sometimes* *often* *usually* *always*

- We use adverbs of frequency with the Present Simple to say how often something happens:
*I **often** go shopping at weekends.*
*She **usually** goes out with her friends on Saturdays.*
- Adverbs of frequency go before most verbs, e.g. *go, see, listen*, etc. but *after* the verb *to be*:
*We **hardly ever go** to the cinema.*
*Andrew **is always** happy.*

Complete the sentences with the pairs of words. Put the verbs in the correct form.

~~never / listen~~ usually / go never / get always / do hardly ever / tidy sometimes / use often / play

1 I *never listen* to classical music.
2 We ______ the Internet for shopping.
3 Natalia ______ her homework on time.
4 They ______ to the beach at weekends.
5 Ricardo ______ football for the school team.
6 We ______ up early on Sundays.
7 You ______ your bedroom.

there is/there are with *some* and *any* → Unit 11, page 40

Use

- We use *there is* and *there are* to say that something is or is not in a particular place:
***There's** a snack bar in the museum.*
***There isn't** a youth club in my town but there are two sports centres.*

- We use ***some*** and ***any*** to talk about an indefinite quantity. We use
– *there is/are some* in affirmative sentences:
There is some *paper in the printer.*
There are some *lifts in the museum.*
– *there isn't/aren't any* in negative sentences and questions:
There isn't any *milk in the fridge.*
There aren't any *spaces in the car park.*
Are there any *cinemas in your town?*

Form

Affirmative	
There's (is) **a** good shopping centre. **There are** some nice snack bars.	
Negative	
There isn't (is not) **an** information centre. **There aren't** (are not) **any** youth clubs.	
Yes/No **questions**	**Short answers**
Is there a cinema? **Are there any** skateparks?	Yes, **there is/are**. No, **there isn't/aren't.**
Wh- **questions**	
What shops **are there**?	

Choose the correct words.

1 There (*'s*)/ *are* a new library in the town centre.
2 There aren't *some / any* sports centres in my town.
3 There *is / are* a lot of cars in the car park.
4 There *isn't / aren't* a swimming pool near my school.
5 There*'s / are* a new tutor at my youth club.
6 There *are / aren't* any good films on at the cinema.
7 There are *some / any* good shops in the new shopping centre.
8 There *isn't / aren't* any English students at my school.

Present Continuous →

Unit 13, page 48; Unit 14, page 50

Use

- We use the Present Continuous to talk about things that are happening now or around now:
I'm standing *in the main street.*
It ***isn't raining****.*
What ***are*** *you* ***doing*** *today?*

- We often use these expressions with the Present Continuous: *now, at the moment, today, this week*:
I'm staying *with my cousins* ***this week****.*

Form

Affirmative				
I He/She/It We/You/They		**'m** (am) **'s** (is) **'re** (are)		**working.***
Negative				
I He/She/It We/You/They		**'m not** (am not) **isn't** (is not) **aren't** (are not)		**working.***
Yes/No **questions**			**Short answers**	
Am **Is** **Are**	I he/she/it we/you/ they	**working?**	Yes, I **am**. Yes, he/she/ it **is.** Yes, we/you/ they **are.**	No, **I'm not**. No, he/she/ it **isn't**. No, we/you/ they **aren't**.
Wh- **questions**				
Where What Why	**am** **is** **are**	I he/she/it we/you/they	**going?** **doing?** **stopping?**	

* Spelling:

Most verbs	+ *ing*	*listen* ***listening***
Verbs ending in a consonant + *e*	take away *e* + *ing*	*drive* ***driving***
One-syllable verb ending in a vowel + a consonant	double the consonant + *ing*	*stop* ***stopping***

1 Complete the sentences with the Present Continuous form of the verbs in the box.

have wear listen ~~drive~~ write sit

1 Ana *is driving* her new car.
2 I ______ to the radio.
3 Lisa and Kim ______ lunch in a café.
4 The cat ______ in front of the fire.
5 Granddad ______ a letter to his friend.
6 You ______ some nice clothes.

2 Write questions and short answers. Use the Present Continuous.

1 you / watch this film? (no)
Are you watching this film?
No, I'm not.
2 your sister / do her homework? (yes)
______
______

3 your friends / play football? (no)

____

____

4 Dad / work in the garden? (yes)

____

____

5 you / use the computer? (no)

____

____

6 it / rain? (yes)

____

____

was / were → Unit 16, page 57

Use

- *was/were* is the past form of *am/is/are*. We use *was/were* for past situations or actions:
Apollo 13 ***was*** *a mission to the Moon.*
I ***was*** *at home yesterday morning.*
- We use *there was/were* as the past form of *there is/are*:
There was *an explosion on the spaceship.*
There weren't *any people in the park.*

Form

Affirmative		
I/He/She/It You/We/They	**was** **were**	cold.
There There	**was** **were**	a problem. three astronauts.
Negative		
I/He/She/It You/We/They	**wasn't** (was not) **weren't** (were not)	comfortable.
There There	**wasn't** (was not) **weren't** (were not)	any food. five astronauts.

Yes/No questions			Short answers	
Was **Were**	I/he/she/it you/we/they	hot?	Yes, I/he/she/it **was**. Yes, you/we/they **were**.	No, I/he/she/it **wasn't**. No, you/we/they **weren't**.
Was **Were**	there there	any water? a lot of problems?	Yes, there **was**. Yes, there **were**.	No, there **wasn't**. No, there **weren't**.

Wh- questions			
Where	**was** **were**	I/he/she/it you/we/they	yesterday?

Complete the dialogue with *was*, *were*, *wasn't*, or *weren't*.

A Why [1] *weren't* you at Emma's party last weekend? [2] ________ you ill?

B No, I [3] ________ . I [4] ________ on holiday with my family. We [5] ________ in Turkey.

A [6] ________ the weather good?

B Yes, it [7] ________ warm and sunny. What about Emma's party? [8] ________ there a lot of people there?

A Yes, there [9] ________ . And the music [10] ________ great.

Past Simple → Unit 17, page 58; Unit 19, page 66; Unit 20, page 68

Use

- We use the Past Simple to talk about finished actions and situations in the past:

NOW

PAST ←——×——┊——————→ FUTURE

We ***crossed*** *Australia by car last year.*
Our train ***didn't arrive*** *on time.*
Did *you* ***go*** *to London last month?*
- We often use a time expression with the Past Simple, e.g. *yesterday, last week, in 2005, this morning* (when it is now, the afternoon or evening):
We went to the beach ***yesterday****.*

Form

There are two types of verb: regular and irregular.

Regular verbs

Affirmative			
I/You/He/She/It/We/They		**worked***	yesterday.
Negative			
I/You/He/She/It/We/They	**didn't** (did not)	**work**	yesterday.

Yes/No questions			Short answers
Did	I/you/he/she/it/we/they	**work**?	Yes, I/you/he/she/it/we/they **did**. No, I/you/he/she/it/we/they **didn't**.

Wh- questions				
Where	**did**	I/you/he/she/it/we/they	**work**	yesterday?

* Spelling:

Most verbs	+ *ed*	*return*	***returned***
Verbs ending in *e*	+ *d*	*arrive*	***arrived***
Verbs ending in *y*	change *y* to *i* and + *ed*	*carry*	***carried***
Travel	double the *l* + *ed*	*travel*	*travel**led***
One-syllable verbs ending in a vowel and a consonant	double the consonant + *ed*	*stop*	***stopped***

Irregular verbs

- Irregular verbs have a different form in the past simple:
go → ***went*** *buy* → ***bought*** *think* → ***thought***
See the Irregular verbs list in the Student's Book page 129.
- We use *did* and *didn't* to form questions and negatives:
*Where **did** you **go** yesterday?*
*I bought a T-shirt but I **didn't buy** a jacket.*

1 Write pairs of sentences. Use the Past Simple.

1 we / see a film (✗) / see a play (✓)
We didn't see a film. We saw a play.

2 they / go to the ice rink (✗) / go to the bowling alley (✓)
____

3 you / come home at 11 (✗) / come home at 11.30 (✓)
____

4 I / meet my friends in town (✗) / meet them at the beach (✓)
____

5 Teresa / send me an email (✗) / send me a text (✓)
____

6 Mr Clarke / teach us geography (✗) / teach us history (✓)
____

2 Write questions for the answers.

1 *What did you have for lunch?*
I had a sandwich and an apple for lunch.

2 ________________
We went to the cinema on Saturday.

3 ________________
Dad went to work at eight o'clock.

4 ________________
Mum went to bed early because she was ill.

5 ________________
I met my best friend in 1998.

6 ________________
We travelled to London by train.

Comparatives and superlatives

→ **Unit 22, page 74**

Use

- We use comparative adjectives to compare two people, places or things. We use *than* after a comparative adjective:
*My sister is **older than** me.*
- We use superlative adjectives to compare three or more people, places or things. We usually use *in*, not *of*, after a superlative adjective:
*It's the biggest **animal in the world**. NOT 'of the world'*
*She's the best **student in the class**. NOT 'of the class'*

Form

Adjective		Comparative	Superlative
one syllable			
old	+ *er* /+ *est*	older	**the oldest**
safe	+*r* / + *st*	safer	**the safest**
big	double consonant after short vowels	bigger	**the biggest**
two syllables ending in *y*			
funny	change *y* to *i* and + *er* / + *est*	funnier	**the funniest**
two or more syllables			
boring	+ *more* / + *the most*	**more** boring	**the most** boring
interesting		**more** interesting	**the most** interesting
beautiful		**more** beautiful	**the most** beautiful
Irregular			
good	—	**better**	**the best**
bad	—	**worse**	**the worst**

1 Correct the underlined mistakes in the sentences.

1 My grandmother is <u>the most oldest</u> person in my family. *the oldest*
2 I think whales are the most interesting animals <u>of</u> the world. ________
3 Adam is <u>happyer</u> at his new school. ________
4 The birds were <u>the noisier</u> animals in the zoo. ________
5 I think skiing is <u>the more dangerous</u> than cycling. ________
6 You were <u>the better</u> player in the team. ________
7 My brother is a lot <u>tallest</u> than me. ________
8 Our new house is <u>biger</u> than our old flat. ________

2 Complete the text with the correct form of the adjectives in brackets.

I had [1] *the best* (good) birthday of my life! We went to the new adventure park – it's [2] ________ (good) than the old park. It's [3] ________ (big) and [4] ________ (exciting). The park has got [5] ________ (high) slide in England. The only problem is that the tickets are [6] ________ (expensive) than before.

In the evening, my friends and I went to my favourite snack bar. We were [7] ________ (noisy) people in the restaurant!

going to → Unit 23, page 76

Use

- We use *going to* + infinitive to talk about plans and intentions for the future:

PAST ←——————— NOW ✕ ———————→ FUTURE

I'm going to *see a film tomorrow.*
We're going to *go shopping next weekend.*

- We often use a time expression with *going to*, e.g. *tomorrow, next week, at the weekend* (when it is now earlier in the week), *this summer* (when it is now earlier in the year):
Are *you* ***going to*** *get a holiday job* ***this summer****?*

Form

Affirmative			
I He/She/It We/You/They	**'m** (am) **'s** (is) **'re** (are)	**going to**	**work**.
Negative			
I He/She/It We/You/They	**'m not** (am not) **isn't** (is not) **aren't** (are not)	**going to**	**work**.

***Yes/No* questions**				**Short answers**	
Am	I	**going to**	**be late?**	Yes, I **am**.	No, I**'m not**.
Is	he/she/it			Yes, he/she/it **is**.	No, he/she/it **isn't**.
Are	we/you/they			Yes, we/you/they **are**.	No, we/you/they **aren't**.

***Wh-* questions**			
What	**are** you	**going to**	**do** this weekend?

1 Write pairs of sentences. Use *going to*.

1 We / play tennis ✗ / go shopping ✓
We aren't going to play tennis. We're going to go shopping.

2 I / watch TV ✗ / do my homework ✓
____

3 Clara / come to the park ✗ / go to the beach ✓
____

4 You / fail the exam ✗ / pass ✓
____

5 Sue and Tim / cook dinner ✗ / go to a restaurant ✓
____

6 We / drive to the coast ✗ / take the train ✓
____

7 Daniel / be a teacher ✗ / study medicine ✓
____

8 it / be sunny ✗ / rain ✓
____

2 Complete the dialogue with the correct form of the verbs in brackets. Use *going to*.

A What [1] *are you going to do* (you / do) at the weekend?

B I [2] ________ (spend) Saturday with my sister. We [3] ________ (meet) in London for the day.

A What sights [4] ________ (you / see)?

B The London Eye and Covent Garden. What about you?

A My parents [5] ________ (not be) at home so I [6] ________ (have) a party on Saturday.

B Great! Who [7] ________ (you / invite)?

A All my friends from school. You can come, too, of course.

B Thanks, but I [8] ________ (not be) free on Saturday evening.

A [9] ________ (you / stay) in London?

B No, I'm not. I [10] ________ (visit) my grandparents.